THE GOD MADE MAN

MADE FOR A GOD MADE LIFE

BOBBY RICE

I dedicate this book to my dad, Bobby J Rice Sr., my father, my hero, and a great example of how to love and follow Christ. It is from him that I learned my greatest life lessons which I share in this book. My dad was the first God Made man in my life.

ABOUT THE COVER

This book will be controversial in today's culture. It wasn't my intention but the subject matter flies in the face of today's popular beliefs. It's biblically truthful. Most will find it challenging. Some may not like it. Knowing the content was "edgy" I wanted a book cover that would match. So, I was at a minor league hockey game in El Paso one night with a friend, a lady, when my publisher sent the original cover art. I showed it to her and we both had the same reaction. It was good, but didn't say exactly what we wanted for the book. So, she turned to me with the most fascinating suggestion, and then proceeded to describe the cover as you see it now. It was one of those "God downloads" right there in El Paso Texas. Her idea was perfect! Right then, I realized I was experiencing the very concept I hold to be true inside the pages of this book. This book would not exist without a man. Yet, it would not matter without a woman. I hope you enjoy.

PREFACE

This is not another "how to be a good husband or how to have a good marriage" book. I've had two failed marriages. I would be the first to ask "who am I to write a book on marriage?" There are plenty of those out there, this is not one of them. Although this book was born out of what I believe God taught me about myself from my two failed marriages, it is much more basic than a "how to" relationship and marriage book. It's a nuts and bolts, core fundamentals book about manhood based on the words of God from the very beginning of it all, Genesis 1, 2, and 3. This is a book about being a God Made Man based on God and Adam's relationship. This book needed to be written and I believe every man needs to read it! Therefore, my primary audience is men.

After my second failed marriage I turned my attention to God and me. No one else. I needed answers about myself. So I began to pray and read like a man desperate for answers. As a man, I wanted to know what God says to and about me. Through my time spent seeking Him, He systematically began to lead me to the beginning of it all, the creation story and more specifically the story of God and Adam.

As I studied what God says about men I quickly realized that understanding God's intentions for men would have to include God's created intentions for women. Eve was created for Adam. Therefore, for Adam to understand his purpose he must understand God's purpose for her in his life as well. As God began to teach me about men it became clear the God Made Man must understand the God Made Woman. I want to restate what I said earlier, this is not a book about how to be a good, supportive, loving and caring wife. That is not what God covers with Eve, but He does cover the same thing we see with Adam, the basic core fundamentals of what His created purpose for all women are. This must be addressed because of the importance in God's original plan and purpose for Adam's life, therefore Eve's.

As I continued my personal journey of seeking God and finding answers for myself, I started thinking about all that God was teaching me. Around the spring of 2021 I began to look back over my notes and journaling and thought, "this could be a book." I started praying about that, and I soon realized this was the new direction God was leading me in.

As a Christian and pastor for many years, and after learning about myself and what God was teaching me for the past three months, and like so many like me who are deeply concerned with our current culture, God began to write this book in my heart. I first had to accept my own failures in my two marriages. I listened to everything God was saying to me about me. I began to study the first three chapters of Genesis. And with the help of others, I'll mention later, it became clear, I have never fully understood until now what it is to be a real man, a God Made Man.

I soon realized this was not only my problem but every man's problem. Then I began to see that, like Adam, I and every man is responsible for the culture God has placed us in. As good common-sense Christian people, we believe God is the answer and has the answers to everything. We believe those answers are found in His Word. If that's so, then back to God's word we must go. That's what I did and it has profoundly changed my life as a man. I believe the answers to our cultural dilemma, the culture of our marriage and homes, and the culture of society is found in what God originally says about men. That's where it begins. But it also includes what God says about women because Eve and her purpose is covered as well. This is what I attempt to do in "The God Made Man." I believe it starts with men being who God made us to be.

Throughout this book I will share my personal experiences in the hope that my story may help some who read this. I've included some of my personal journaling that covers the greatest lessons learned to date in my life. Most importantly, I will share what God is teaching me through His word. I believe our culture can be changed for the good. But no change will happen until men rediscover what it is to be a God Made Man.

CULTURE SHAPERS

The God Made Man, The God Made Woman, and The God Made Marriage were made to influence, form, and shape our culture. Sociology defines culture as "the total of the inherited ideas, beliefs, values, and knowledge, which constitute the shared bases of social action. It is the attitudes, feelings, values, and behavior that characterize and inform society as a whole or any social group within it." Culture is not supposed to shape us. As men and women made in God's image we hold the power of influence and it is our responsibility to shape our culture as God shapes us. As you will see, Adam was placed in the garden to reign over, subdue, and influence every living thing. He was created for and taught how to shape its culture.

What you are about to read was born out of an intense time of seeking God for myself. As I'm in my senior years, I wasn't ready to give up on living and fade away. I know there is more for me to do. But I needed answers. As a Christian man, my second failed marriage rattled my cage. I honestly asked God and myself, "why am I the way I am? Why do I relate to others the way I do?" God did for me what He'll do for anyone who honestly and earnestly seeks Him. He will meet you where you are and He will teach you. Chapters 9 & 10, my journaling, are literally what I believe God revealed to me about myself. It was needed, it was a blessing, and it has changed my life. I included it in hopes it will help someone who reads it. It may be necessary for some to jump to those chapters first. Chapter 9 is about my struggles with bitterness, anger, and unforgiveness. This was the first thing I spent time on with God. You will not be who God made you to be if you're holding onto bitterness and unforgiveness toward someone in your life, past or present. Chapter 10 is about the greatest most liberating lessons God has taught me to date about myself; the emotional wounds I received from my father and mother. The truth is, we all carry wounds of some kind and they shape our relationship behaviors. So, it may not be a bad idea to start with those chapters before chapter 1. You prayerfully decide. Throughout each chapter you will hear me challenge and encourage men to put God first in their lives, know His word, and be the men God made us to be. This is the thrust of this book.

I want you to take a journey with me through Genesis 1, 2, and 3 the creation story. This is what I've done, again, and it has profoundly changed my life. Men, the answers to "The God Made Man" are in that story. Let's get started.

Remember, this is not a "marriage book." Although I talk about Adam and Eve and my two marriages, I am hopefully helping readers avoid the mistakes and choices I made. I encourage you to focus on the "building blocks, the fundamentals" of what God is teaching men about how to be a real authentic man. The answer to authentic God Made Men is there in your Bible in the story of God, Adam, and Eve.

INTRODUCTION

THE GOD MADE MAN

God made men to be committed followers of Him and strong courageous leaders in the <u>culture</u> in which you are placed. This is the heart and desire of God from the beginning for all men. This hasn't changed! Our culture desperately needs authentic men. Men need to learn the timeless biblical truths that will set or reset the course of their life to the right path. The God Made Man came from what God has been teaching me through the many intense hours of spending time with Him. Therefore, I will be challenging men throughout each chapter to be the men God made us to be.

In Genesis 4:10, God said this to Cain after he murdered his brother, *"And the LORD said, 'What have you done? The voice of your brother's blood is crying to me from the ground.'"* Able's death needed reconciling, so God goes to the offender. Our culture needs reconciling because it is so far from God that it's crying out for change. It must be turned back to God! That "turning back" will happen when men live again as the men God made us to be.

WE NEED MEN OF STRENGTH

One of my favorite quotes from John Wayne is, "You have to be a man first before you can be a gentleman," as the character McLintock.

I took a part-time job working for the John Wayne family in Fort Worth, Texas. Ethan Wayne, John Wayne's youngest son—you'll remember him as the young grandson who was kidnapped in *Big Jake*—opened a John Wayne museum in the Stockyards of Ft. Worth Texas. Aside from the people I love, preaching, teaching and writing, this has become one of the joys of my life. Not only are the Wayne family great people, I also get to meet true, good, common sense people every day. If I hear this statement once I hear it a dozen times a week, "we need more people like John Wayne today." Or, "I wish he was alive today." If you're a John Wayne fan and concerned about the culture, you know what they mean. In the mind of all John Wayne fans, he was a man's man, a strong man, a real man. Boys wanted to be like him and girls wanted to marry a man like him. Those were the characters he played on the big screen—real, strong, caring, coura- geous men. These comments are made by people like me who aren't happy with the current state of affairs in our culture. So, when I hear people say those things, my reply is, "let's you and I make a John Wayne difference in our culture." When I issue that challenge, most will give an affirming head nod or say, "You're right."

We need men of strength and courage today. It's easy to look around at our culture and think "we've lost, it's too far gone." But, brothers, it's not! It is however going to take change. Sometimes it seems overwhelming when we look at how far left and further away from God the culture has moved. Our country is not the God-fearing nation it once was. But it's not lost, and this nation, our values, our families, goodness, and righteousness can be reclaimed again. It must start with men being the men God made us to be. Our culture makes that seem impossible, but God and His word say it can happen, it must happen. As one man I cannot bring sweeping change to an entire country, but I can bring sweeping change to my life, my relationships, family, and the culture in which God has placed me, and so can you. It must start with individual men turning to God and being the men He created us to be. I believe the answers to our cultural dilemma are found in what God originally said about men, so we must return to God's word. And we must return now!

ONLY GOD CAN MAKE A MAN READY

Adam had the same experience at being a husband as every single man who has never been married had… NONE. Neither did Adam have the unfortunate experiences that too many of us have had, being raised in a dysfunctional world and quite possibly in a dysfunctional home. It is true, we are the product of our raising. Sadly, some of our parents were not always the best teachers and examples. Now I know some of us can say we had wonderful fathers and mothers. I'm happy for you. Some can say one or the other parent was wonderful, and some will say neither were. These life experiences strongly influence our beliefs. This is why it's so important to look at God and Adam's life before and after Eve to learn the biblical principles for all men that are found in Adam's and God's relationship. Traditionally, we enter into marriage as young adults. Adam and Eve were probably young adults, but their relationship had something that every good and successful marriage must have: A husband with a firm foundation that comes from time spent with God. It was Adam, the man, the husband that God spent time with in preparation for his life. Adam was made ready for Eve. It is God that did the preparing of Adam, and it is God that chose the exact time to make and bring him his Eve.

I remember clearly in 1974 when I was a junior in high school and already giving serious thought to who my wife would be. I know that sounds strange but that was me. I had a strong since that I would be married young, probably out of high school. I can remember teaching the high school Sunday school class one Sunday at my father's church while in high school myself and asking those students to pray for me and my "search". At 17 I was clearly not ready but I was mentally and prayerfully in pursuit of her. I met the mother of our two sons in the summer of 1975 the year I graduated high school. We married in December of the same year. Young and naive, there I was a married man without a clue. Now many years later I'm looking back over two failed marriages wishing I knew then what I know now. I know, there's so much of life and making mistakes that simply has to be lived and experienced.

Every man young and old can learn the lesson of being prepared by God as Adam was because we have His word, our Bible. There is no better time than now to learn these important and timeless biblical truths. It is my prayer that men, young and old, will learn the priceless value of being prepared by God. My hope is that you will be challenged and encouraged through the words of this book. My goal is to share everything God is teaching me. I will be honest and open with you about my life experiences, failures, and successes. Hopefully you will hear something that will encourage you to truly make God priority NUMBER ONE in your life. As a man, your life, your relationships, your home, your vocation, and your culture are depending on it.

CHAPTER 1

WHAT HAPPENED TO AUTHEN-TIC MANHOOD?

What happened to men who at their core believe in doing what's right and then doing it? Men who honor God and respect others. Men who love and honor their wives. One of my favorite and most challenging verses of scripture has always been James 4:17, [17] *"Remember, it is sin to know what you ought to do and then not do it."* Ladies, does your man open doors for you? Does he pull out your chair to seat you first? Does he stand when you enter the room? Does he walk on the curb side of the side walk so you're not next to the traffic? There should never come a time when a lady is not treated with this kind of respect. A God Made Man knows how important his wife is to him and will show her honor. But, it's so much more than chivalry. A God Made Man knows God, puts God first in his life, before all others, and keeps Him there.

. . .

A GOD MADE MAN IS A HERO

Do you remember your boyhood heroes? Mine were men like Matt Dillon, Ben Cartwright, GI Joe, John Wayne, and Clark Kent. These are the men I grew up admiring. I have a scar under my chin as a result of imitating Superman one Saturday morning with a towel for a cape around my neck leaping from the piano to the sofa but coming up short on the edge of the coffee table. I wanted to be like him. He was a man with more than super powers. He was a good, decent, fair, kind, just, and STRONG man.

I'm blessed to have had a father who was my hero, my real-life Superman. My dad played endless hours of catch with me and my brother. He taught us how to fish. He bought us our first shotguns when we were 11 & 12 years old and he taught us how to safely use them. I still have that single shot 410 from Sears and Roebucks, what a treasure.

I remember when I was eight, Dad came home from work one day to hang a rope and tire swing in the big oak tree. He was an electrician and wore blue jeans with the cuffs rolled up, a smudged white tee shirt from working all day and he smelled like work. When he came home that day, he reached into the back of his work truck and pulled out a long fat rope he picked up from the shipyard and an old tire. But what he did next solidified his hero status in my eight-year-old heart. He strapped on a leather harness with metal buckles and spikes on his boots and up that tree he went, jamming those boot spikes into the tree, pulling that heavy rope up with him. I watched with excitement and AWE as he crawled out on the limb and tied and wired that rope to the limb. Then down the tree he came jamming one boot spike at a time in the side of that tree. I'll never forget that, and I told all my buddies at school about it.

We need real authentic strong men today. Men that other men and boys can look up to. Men who aren't afraid of doing the right thing because the right thing is the right thing to do. Honest men. Men who know to whom they are accountable. Brothers, there's the key. Every man must know to whom he is accountable first and before all others; He is God! My dad was that kind of man and God shaped his life and therefore mine. I should say here, dad was far from perfect, but in my young eyes he was flawless.

WE MUST COME BACK TO GOD

Men, if we are accountable to God our creator then we must come back to Him. We must seek Him and He must be priority number one in our lives. Hebrews 4:12-13 says, *"For the word of God is alive and powerful. It is sharper than the sharpest two-edged sword, cutting between soul and spirit, between joint and marrow. It exposes our innermost thoughts and desires. Nothing in all creation is hidden from God. Everything is naked and exposed before his eyes, and he is the one to whom we are accountable."* Men, we are accountable to God first, before anyone, even your wife, your family, career, and anything else!

Before I go further I want to explain what's about to be said and why. It's going to sound like I'm speaking against the gospel; I am not! I am though, going to express my thoughts about what we've done to the gospel. When I use the word "gospel" I'm not talking only about the first four books of the new testament, I'm talking about the whole truth of God's word. The pure message of the Bible hasn't changed and never will. Sadly, we have done the changing and, men, I put us at the top of the blame list. So, I warn you in case you have those sensitivities. Men, I want you to see this and feel this. I want you to hear the knock of urgency at your door. We were created to be culture shapers and we must step back into that role again.

The reason our culture is in the shape it's in is because Christians are living what I call a "pansy ass weak gospel." It is because the powerful life changing gospel truth is not being lived confidently and boldly with authority BY MEN!

Families are decimated and as a result boys don't know how to be boys; girls don't know how to be girls. Gender is confused by the twisted evil messages of our culture. Men don't know how to be strong men (refer back to the boy problem), women don't know how to be confident feminine women (refer back to the girl problem). Never before in my lifetime has there been so much confusion about sexuality and gender. I raised two sons. If at any time they would've expressed their confusion about who and what they were, I would've taken them to the bathroom and the three of us would stand before the mirror. Then I'd say "let's get naked boys I want to explain something." I'd point and say, "you see that, you are a boy, only boys have one of those and one day you'll grow up to be a man. And, God made you to like girls A LOT!" Now, I know that's oversimplifying it in the light of our crazy culture but I ask you, where did we go wrong? It's when men stopped being the authentic men God made us to be.

Marriages are a disaster. Husbands don't know their God given places so they struggle to lead with confidence, strength, and love. Wives have abandoned their God given places to follow and honor their husbands. 1st Corinthians 13, "the love chapter", is spoken about and desired in marriage, but too many husbands and wives don't understand the message of the love chapter and sure don't know how to love, show love, give love, and receive love. We know about it, but we don't know how to live it. Here's why, too many Christian men and women have drifted away from the core truth of God's word. I could go on about the culture, schools, business, and government but you get the picture. WHAT'S THE SOLUTION? Being the men God made us to be! Men, we must allow God to show us our failures. And we must repent.

As I look back over my years of living on this earth, most of my life as a Christian and the majority of those years as a committed follower of Jesus, a pastor for twenty-seven years, and a serious student of the Bible, I believe the problem is clear.

OUR LAYERS OF BELIEF

THE PROBLEM is that a weak Gospel is being lived because a weak gospel is being preached, taught, and counseled in the church. Here's what I mean. The plain spoken, clearly written word of God has been dumbed down and filtered through our own perceptions and thoughts. I call them our layers of weak belief that have over time developed in us. The right thing goes unsaid or is softened because we're afraid we might hurt feelings. Especially when it comes to the man and woman's role. Too many preachers, pastors, and teachers are afraid to preach the clear word of God. That's not what the Prophets did in the Old Testament. That's not what Jesus did in the Gospels. And that's not what Paul did to the churches. The church got its powerful and mighty start because God the Holy Spirit did just what God said He was going to do. The church was founded on the rock solid uncompromising word of God.

The TRUTH about God the Father, God the Son, God the Holy Spirit, the church, the truth about sin, right and wrong, men and women, marriage and family, needs to be declared. DECLARE IT and let the powerful truth of God's Word sort it out and sort us out. I'm writing to the people who God created to be culture shapers; the God Made Man.

I want to be very clear. The Gospel, God's word, is not weak! It is us and the way we believe and live that weakens its message. It is what I call, as I have mentioned, layers upon layers of accumulated wrong belief passed down through the centuries. For centuries people have been putting their own spin on the Bible. They put their layer of understanding on it and the layers pile high and go deep. We need to take an axe to the root of our layers and let God's truth stand and change our lives.

. . .

THE PRACTICE OF SUBTLE MANIPULATION

Here's why a weak gospel is lived. In the church, the Christian community is guilty of placing layer upon layer of their own self-perceived, self understood "truth" on the simple but powerful Word of God. It's the subtle seduction and practice of saying "this is what _I think_ God is saying to me, or this is what _I think_ God is saying about this." And to you and even others it sounds good but it's just a little off. When you compare what some say to the plain spoken word of God, it's simply incorrect. God's word is never "close" and is never "off" by any degree. It's here that some will say, "It's arrogant to say you can know for sure what God is saying." But it's not arrogant. When God is truly first in your life and when you have prioritized your relationship with God you will know His truth! God will see to it. Adam knew God's truth for himself. So can we.

This practice of subtle manipulation of God's truth began in the garden when the Serpent deceived Eve. He gave her another way of looking at the truth and she, like so many of us, accepted a new belief. Her different belief became her layer. It was another way of looking at it, yet it was opposite from what God said. Her layer made sense to her as ours makes sense to us.

Listen men, because you need to get this. Satan's target was not Eve. His target was always Adam and God. He went through Eve to destroy God's plan for Adam. It worked! Men, here's a truth that you must know and clearly understand; Satan hates you because you are a man! But it's more than that. He knows that from the beginning God laid the foundation and placed responsibility on men to be His first image bearer. The man is to love, lead, guide, shape, and protect his home as God leads him. Men are to lead their wives with respectful love and authority. And wives are to follow, honor, and love their husbands. Satan knows all about God's plan and purpose for men. Satan knows you are to be strong mighty men in the world God has placed you in. Ever since creation, Satan has been trying to reverse what God has created. He successfully deceived Eve to get to Adam and to destroy God's plan, and Satan is successfully doing it today, sadly.

In the Old Testament and those 400 years between the testaments before Jesus, we see the practice of layering turn into an all-out assault on God's word by the Jewish religious leaders as they, for centuries, added law upon law, regulation upon regulation, layer upon layer of their own belief on God's word making it impossible to follow and distorting its purity. As a result, the generation that Jesus was born into believed that these men were Holy men.

We've been seeing this ramp up today in the evangelical church ever since the Pentecostal movement in the early 1900s. We call some of the craziest things in the church the "work of the Holy Spirit," and it's nothing but man induced layers. It started as a slow drifting away from the plain, direct, simple truth as people began to leave sound doctrine and place more emphasis and importance on emotion and feeling which is where Satan loves to play. Then the reform and human rights movements began. Although I believe this was needed and many good and needed changes came from this, it has evolved into the emasculation of our culture and now a lawlessness like the world has never seen.

The Bible is filled with great examples of Godly, Manly, Strong men. To name a few, Adam, Moses, King David, Apostle Paul, and Peter. History records many more strong men that God used. Men like, George Whitefield, Dietrich Bonhoeffer, Billy Graham, and many others. Sadly today we are witnessing what I believe Satan's goal is, to cause a strong society which should be led by strong men to become weak and without strength of character. This was Satan's goal with Adam and Eve in the beginning and he hasn't stopped.

This is what Satan did to Eve. He appealed to her feelings and emotions. People today are more concerned about what a preacher or teacher says about a thing than what the Bible says about it. I always encouraged the churches I pastored to check what I preached and taught through their Bible. Too many people today are more connected to emotions and feelings that are stirred in them from music, lights, and smoke than wether or not the message and lyrics are biblical. The Bible says this in 2 Timothy 4:2-4, *"preach the word; be ready in season and out of season; reprove, rebuke, and exhort, with complete patience and teaching. For the time is coming when people will not endure sound teaching, but having itching ears they will accumulate for themselves teachers to suit their own passions, and will turn away from listening to the truth and wander off into myths."* So now, in too many churches, biblical truth is distorted and deformed by the layer upon layer of what sounds like and feels like the right thing. A simple check of God's word would shed a beam of light on the error and reveal the truth. What has evolved in the TV and mega church culture and many smaller churches *(not all are this way)* is a weak Bible message. Weak and power-less full of emotion that people believe is right, and they believe it's "God's presence." People flock to it like bugs to light at night. But in fact it's a "form of the right thing" that stirs our emotions to the point we now say "it must be God." Men, we need to be men of THE BIBLE! Your leadership in this has always been needed and more so today.

WE MUST GO TO THE BEGINNING

Where do we go? Where is the answer? I believe the answer is found in the beginning? I'm talking about Genesis 1-3, that beginning. Jesus knew it as well, let me show you. The people of Jesus's day were living under the heavy burden of their own layers of belief. So much so they had forgotten the very words and teaching of God and were consumed with the teachings of the rabbis rather than what God originally said. The answer is where God speaks first and specifically about manhood, in the beginning.

Let me prove this. Back to the beginning is where Jesus directed His listeners when He was confronted by "religious leaders." Their question was about divorce and the teaching of Moses on the subject. But Jesus does what we must all do; He goes back to what God said in the beginning. For Jesus, the answer to man and woman is found in the original words of God in the beginning. In Matthew 19:1-8 it says, *[1] When Jesus had finished saying these things, he left Galilee and went down to the region of Judea east of the Jordan River. [2] Large crowds followed him there, and he healed their sick. [3] Some Pharisees came and tried to trap him with this question: "Should a man be allowed to divorce his wife for just any reason?" [4] "Haven't you read the Scriptures?" Jesus replied. "They (the scriptures) record that from the beginning 'God made them male and female.'" [5] And he said, "'This explains why a man leaves his father and mother and is joined to his wife, and the two are united into one.' [6] Since they are no longer two but one, let no one split apart what God has joined together." [7] "Then why did Moses say in the law that a man could give his wife a written notice of divorce and send her away?" they asked. [8] Jesus replied, "Moses permitted divorce only as a concession to your hard hearts, but it was not what God had originally intended. (NKJ says, "but from the beginning it was not so.")*

When it comes to basic understanding of biblical truth concerning men and women the answers are found in what God said in the beginning, and Jesus knew it. Jesus is talking about PRE-FALL BEGINNING. If you want to discover what and who a real man and woman is meant to be you must go to the beginning. If you want answers to the cultural problems today you must go to what God originally said about a man and woman. The answers are there. If you want to understand AUTHENTIC MANHOOD, we must go back to what God said about men in the beginning. Books about manhood, womanhood, and marriage are abundant on store book shelves. Many are worth your time to read but none trump what God said. No matter what you're going through now, the answer is found in what God says about you in the beginning. Men, if the answers are found in the beginning then there is where we as men must go. I don't know how else to say it.

A WORD OF CAUTION

A word of caution here, men. It can be a scary thing for some women when men seek to be strong godly men. For some women, the teaching of pre-fall manhood found in Genesis is outdated and irrelevant in today's culture. Let's face it, today's culture does consider biblical teaching about men and women irrelevant which is the reason we must return. During my separation, my own personal experience was hearing my wife tell me that "my position on Adam was all wrong." I had not yet shared with her what I'd been learning. All she knew at the time was that I was studying it for myself and that was a threat to her. Some women are threatened by what God says a man should be. Maybe they've had bad experiences with abusive men. Or some have never had strong confident loving men in their lives. So, for some women, a strong godly man who leads as God leads him is scary to them because they've never known it. Nevertheless, when men and women are as God says we should be it will change the culture of your life. And that's what's needed today!

This is of paramount importance to men, but it's what most men miss. I'll explain. Let's look at Mark 12:29, Jesus said this, *"The most important commandment is this: 'Listen, O Israel! The LORD our God is the one and only LORD."* Jesus was referring to Exodus 20:1-6 when He said this. This is what I love about studying the Bible. A simple reference search of your study Bible will tell you Jesus is referring to the first commandment of the Ten Commandments. *[1] Then God gave the people all these instructions: [2] "I am the LORD your God, who rescued you from the land of Egypt, the place of your slavery. [3] "You must not have any other god but me. [4] "You must not make for yourself an idol of any kind or an image of anything in the heavens or on the earth or in the sea. [5] You must not bow down to them or worship them, for I, the LORD your God, am a jealous God who will not tolerate your affection for any other gods. I lay the sins of the parents upon their children; the entire family is affected-even children in the third and fourth generations of those who reject me. [6] But I lavish unfailing love for a thousand generations on those who love me and **obey my commands."***

Men, if Jesus tells us that God is to be before anyone and anything, and if Jesus tells us to go back to the beginning, then that's what we must do. Mark 12:30 says, *"And you must love the LORD your God with all your heart, all your soul, all your mind, and all your strength."* MEN MUST PUT GOD FIRST! Three of my favorite Bible teachers today are John Piper, David Jeremiah, and Trampus Black. I'll refer to these men and how they have influenced me as we go.

David Jeremiah in his book "Forward" talks about the lesson he learned 55 years earlier in his life and ministry. He had just started a new church and in his young zeal he worked hard at building this new church utilizing every spare minute of his days. He had a young wife and two small children. He tells the story of how he would come home for dinner and then go back to knocking on as many doors as he could all in hopes of reaching people and growing his new church. One day, after his wife talked to him about spending more time with church work and neglecting his family, he refocused and reprioritized his life. In the early days of his ministry he committed his life to these four priorities.

1. I am a **person** with a responsibility to God.

2. I am a **partner** with a responsibility to my wife.

3. I am a **parent** with a responsibility to my kids.

4. I am a **pastor** with a responsibility to my congregation.

FOCUS AND PRIORITY

Men, you can have the right priorities in your life but if you don't focus on each one, these priorities will get scrambled. Here's the thing, no Christian can argue that this is not the correct order of priority. The Bible teaches it. The thing that causes men so many problems is we don't get the first responsibility right in our lives and keep it. We don't spend the time with God and make Him first as He requires of us. We move on to trying to be a good husband, a good parent, and a good vocationalist. As a result, our marriages are a wreck and too often end in divorce, children are messed up for life, and we never find peace in our vocations. All because men fail to get the first responsibility, *you and God* right so the rest fail. You and God must be and continue to be your first priority. Men must know what God says about them, what He wants for you as a man, and what His purpose and plan is for each of you. This must always be your first and ongoing pursuit. I believe if men will get this priority right the rest will be ordered by God's will. So, here's my question, how much time are you as a man spending with God? Remember there are four priorities in which you must allow God to show you in order to have balance in your life. This is why we must go to the beginning and see what God says about men through Adam's story.

GOING DEEP INTO GOD AND ADAM'S STORY

We're going to consider the time and investment God made with Adam, and Adam with God before Eve, before children, and before Adam's life after the fall. We'll consider the time spent and what God said to Adam after the fall. This is where I believe men and women miss it. Jesus said the first and greatest commandment is, *"Listen, O Israel! The LORD our God is the one and only LORD. And you must love the LORD your God with all your heart, all your soul, all your mind, and all your strength"* Mark 12:29-30.

This is what God established first with Adam. Therefore, He wants the same from each of us. GOD MUST BE FIRST IN YOUR LIFE BEFORE ANYTHING AND ANYONE. We must go back to the beginning to discover it.

When a man puts God first, God makes him a better man and husband. God makes him a better father, and God makes him a better provider. My friend Trampus once asked, and I agree, "Why wouldn't a woman want a man who puts God first?" There's a reason why some women don't want their husbands to make God number one in their lives and I'll share that later.

Our homes and our culture need men who know who they are as God created us to be. There'll be no change until this happens. In the next chapter we're going to do a deep dive into the teachings of the beginning story found in Genesis 1-3. Cinch up! You'll need a tight saddle.

CHAPTER 2

THE GOD MADE MAN PUTS GOD FIRST

I like the term, "masculinity." Masculinity as a noun means virility, strength, toughness, manliness, robustness, and ruggedness. I love that! Stop for a moment and think about this. God created masculinity! And when He made you He made you masculine. John Wayne, in his movie "True Grit", plays a rugged masculine man seeking justice for a young girl. One of my favorite scenes is when he faces four men on horseback, he shouts, "fill your hands you son of a bitch!" He puts the reigns in his mouth, fills both hands with his rifle and revolver, and rides straight into battle. Later in the movie he cradles the young girl in his arms after she's been bitten by a rattlesnake and sacrifices everything to save her life. That's masculinity, strength, and compassion. My prayer for all men is that we step back into our masculine role of doing the right thing, because the right thing is the right thing to do!

. . .

HOW TO BE THE MAN GOD MADE US TO BE

When talking about going back to the beginning to learn about real, authentic manhood, in other words, how to be the man God made us to be today, we literally must go back to Genesis 1-3. It is there that men today will find the answer to what a real man should be. I believe the Bible teaches that God never changes and that He is the same yesterday, today, and forever. I believe in that biblical truth. So, it makes sense that if we want to know what the Bible says about real authentic manhood then we need to go back to what the unchanging God originally said about the first man Adam. For the first time in my life I see it clearly. My hope is that young men won't wait years as I did and that we who are older and wiser will courageously stand strong in our masculine manhood.

In January 2021, I began a deep study of Genesis 1-3 that has changed me profoundly and given me clearer understanding into what a real man should be, the man I should be. Here's how it started. I had already been feeling drawn to study Adam and Eve for some time. In the fall of 2020 I invited a close friend of mine, his name is Trampus Black, to preach at the church I was pastoring. What a name, Trampus, talk about a manly name! Truth is he's one of the manliest men I know. He was part of an end of summer series where I invited different preachers to come, one per month. On this Sunday Trampus preached on the sovereignty of God. As I listened I was spell-bound. He made this statement, it went something like this, "I believe the whole truth of the Bible, the entire gospel message and the answer to humanity, even the answer to today's culture can be found in Genesis 1-3." That statement captured my heart. Few knew at the time that my second marriage of almost seven years was close to ending. I was in an emotional wrestling match with what to do. I had struggled for years with my past and things about me that I didn't have answers for, and I desperately needed answers. So, in January 2021 I began to pray and study Genesis 1, 2, and 3. God began to open my eyes to His truth about me, who I was, why I am the way I am, and His purpose for my life as a man. It was amazing! He was so personal with me and literally opened my eyes to His truths. I can now say with absolute certainty that the answers to what it is to be a man, a real man, are found in the beginning. It is these truths I now want to share with you.

THE ANSWERS ARE FOUND IN THE CREATION STORY

From God's creation story and the creation of Adam and Eve, we find God's purposes and plans for every man and every woman. Please don't miss what I just said. God's purpose and plan for your life is found in the beginning. I know, that was over 6,000 years ago and this is the 21st century, but listen, God never changes. Even though they had a different beginning than the rest of us—they were not birthed, they were formed and made, most likely, as young adults—those biblical truths still remain. In their creation we can clearly see God's intentions for the man and woman today. The way God created them, the order in which He created them (Adam first, Eve second,) the individual responsibilities He gave to each of them, and the way He dealt with them after the fall, all reveals God's plans and purposes for all men and women after Adam and Eve. I'm almost hesitant to move from this point because I want you to grasp the weight and significance of what you just read. The answers to today's man and woman are found in the first three chapters of the Bible. I urge you to hear and grasp this truth.

I think it's important here to talk about the value of understanding "biblical principles." Principles and biblical precepts are throughout the Bible. With Adam, the only thing we cannot relate to is the way he was created. He was "formed" from the dust of the ground a full-grown man. Adam and Eve didn't experience birth and those years of growing to adulthood. You and I were born from the womb of our mother and then grew from infancy, to adolescence, to teens, to adulthood. Everything else about Adam and God are biblical principles and precepts (truths) that we can apply to our lives. They are not direct commands like the Ten Commandments are, but they are biblical truths nonetheless that we must apply to our own lives. So, let's see what God's word says about men. Let's see what God says about you.

CREATED TO BE IMAGE BEARERS

One of the first things we see is this, we were created to be IMAGE BEARERS created in God's image. Not just Adam and Eve but all of us. This is one of those biblical principles that hasn't changed. This was not for Adam only. That's what makes it a biblical principle for us today. Genesis 1:26-27 says, *[26] Then God said, "Let us make human beings in our image, to be like us. They will reign over the fish in the sea, the birds in the sky, the live-stock, all the wild animals on the earth, and the small animals that scurry along the ground." [27] So God created human beings in his own image. In the image of God he created them; male and female he created them."*

A clue to what being "made in God's image" is when God said, *"be like us."* Who? The answer is, God and Jesus. The order and authority of their relationship was God is first Jesus is second, Father and Son. Their Devine relationship is the model for all men. When the order, priority, and focus is as God designed it, we will bare His image.

The second clue is when God said, *"they will reign over."* As God, Jesus, and Holy Spirit reign over all creation, we will reign and have authority over what God has given us. By doing these two things obediently we bare and reflect His image.

Another way that I understand image baring is when I was a boy, I loved playing baseball. One season comes to mind when I was eleven years old in South East Texas. I played for the Pirates. When I put that uniform on, I was a pirate. I was no longer just a boy, my mom and dad's son, I was a little league pirate. I was one of 15 who bore the image of the Pirates. That year we won the championship and with it came a trophy that I proudly displayed in my room. That trophy was the image of what I had accomplished with my team. Just as that uniform and trophy was the image of a championship baseball team, God has made me to be and bare the image of Himself and live as He has created me to live on his team. But the question we all must answer is how else do we bare God's image today?

Like God, we have emotions and feelings. We have a clear sense of right and wrong. God made us that way. We communicate with God and we obey God. But unlike God, we can disobey Him. Unlike the animals, we bare His image to the world. Jesus, in His obedience to the Father represented his Father. As a man I represent my creator. And I represent well when I do it obediently as He designed.

Both Adam and Eve were created in God's image. They were to reflect His image according to His Will, which also means they were to live in the way that he originally designed them to live as a man and a woman. Those same biblical truths haven't changed and are for every man and woman today.

GOD LAYS OUT CLEAR BIBLICAL PRINCIPLES

The way God intended a man to be is found in the Bible, in the creation account. God lays out clear biblical principles about a man. As I began my study of Genesis 1, 2, & 3 I began to realize the authentic strong man for today is found there in the creation account.

A man bares the image of God today by being the man God originally designed men to be. We must be everything God made us to be, not partly, not some, but all. IF THIS WAS GOD'S WILL FOR ADAM THEN THE BIBLICAL PRINCIPLE IS THAT IT IS GOD'S WILL FOR A MAN TODAY. Eve was also made in God's image and for her to fulfill God's purpose as He designed, then like Adam, she must be the woman today as God originally designed. I will say more on the woman's role in the pages to come.

Here's the question: Are we yielded enough to God to allow Him to make us His authentic men where we are in our lives right now? Forget about the clutter and noise that is your life. You, alone dependent on no one else, have the responsibility to reflect who God is by being who God made you to be. In Genesis 2, God created the man to love God first. He is to be in right relationship with God. This means knowing what God wants for you as a man.

Look again at Mark 12:29-30, *[29] Jesus answered him, "The first of all the commandments is: 'Hear, O Israel, the LORD our God, the LORD is one. [30] And you shall love the LORD your God with all your heart, with all your soul, with all your mind, and with all your strength.' This is the first commandment."* Men, I want you to hear what I'm about to say. God's sovereign will was set in motion for all men and women before the first sin.

There are consequences for our choices. It's like the laws of gravity. It won't be altered. The Bible calls it *"sowing and reaping"*(Galatians 6:8). We will reap what we sew. Those are consequences! As I write this I'm at the end of my second marriage. I can't tell you how much this grieves me. I am reaping the consequences of my choices. But it has also driven me to seek God for answers to my life. God really is good to those who seek Him. What He is showing me has been one of the biggest blessings of my life to date. He'll do the same for you. I urge you to seek God just as you are and where you are in your life. He will answer you because He has so much more for you. You are His first image bearer!

GOD'S IMAGE BEARER PUTS HIM FIRST

What does "putting God first" mean and what does it look like? This is where most Christian men miss it BIG TIME because we don't fully understand it. Let's look at God and Adam's life before the fall. It's about time spent with God building relationship with Him. Your relationship with God will never be the number one priority until you focus on it.

I've literally heard all my life about the importance of spending time with God through Bible reading, prayer, and living. I've tried to maintain a consistent fellowship with God, and thought I was, but after studying the life of Adam before the fall I realize God has never been *consistently* first in my life. It was a revolving door relationship with God, in and out. Two failed marriages and the many other family, life, and vocational problems over the years could've been handled better and even avoided if I had maintained my first relationship priority, me and God. My dad used to say, "if you don't feel close to God, who moved?" It is me who would drift away, not God. Don't get me wrong, life will have its share of challenges because we live in a sinful fallen world. But God is a problem solver, and He personally loves each of us. So, let this sink in and make since; as a man, God created you to be in a rich growing relationship with Him that should never end.

THE APPLE OF GOD'S EYE

Adam was created first. God did this on purpose. It was His choice and intention; His plan to create the man first. Today's culture will read this and say, "this proves that God is a chauvinist." No! He's God and He's sovereign. Let's look at the Genesis account and see how important you are as a man to God. Genesis 2:4-7 says, [4] *This is the account of the creation of the heavens and the earth. When the LORD God made the earth and the heavens, [5] neither wild plants nor grains were growing on the earth. For the LORD God had not yet sent rain to water the earth, and there were no people to cultivate the soil. [6] Instead, springs came up from the ground and watered all the land. [7] Then the LORD God formed the man from the dust of the ground. He breathed the breath of life into the man's nostrils, and the man became a living person."* Men, to understand how important you are to God you must see this. Created first doesn't mean you're better than anyone, and it doesn't mean He likes you more than Eve. But order and priority is important to God. In other words, our Holy God did what He did because He is sovereign. And in His sovereignty he says, "this is how I want it to be." We see the principal of God's order and priority throughout the Bible. Everything God does and how He does it should be important to us as His followers. Let's look deeper into Genesis 2:7 and see the divine detail in His creation of Adam, therefore His purpose for men.

Verse 7 says, *"Then the LORD God formed the man from the dust of the ground. He breathed the breath of life into the man's nostrils, and the man became a living person."*

First, understand this, Adam (man), was the first of all breathing beings created with a heart beat in the garden. Men, see this! It was the man that was created first in the order of all living beings. You are important, you are first in the order of things to almighty God. So stand tall, brothers, and be the man God created you to be. God wants all men today to see their importance to Him.

Second, notice the word "formed." Adam was formed from the dust or dirt of the ground. That word "formed" is the same biblical word that describes what a potter does with his hands. A potter will place a clump of moist clay on his wheel and begin to carefully shape and form it from the plan that's in his mind using the pressure of his hands, adding water as needed, to carefully bring the form into shape. God didn't place his hands on wet dirt and say, "let's see what we can make of this." Adam's image was in God's mind before He put His hands on the dirt. The first image bearer was created uniquely and purposefully different from Eve. There's a huge significance in this that we'll see in the pages to come.

Third, when Adam had been fully formed he lay

there lifeless on the ground. And then God did something that He only did for Adam. He doesn't do this to the animals nor to Eve. He breathed the breath of HIS LIFE into Adam's nostrils. I believe the literal breath of God was breathed into Adam's nostrils by God and filled his body with Himself. Notice the intimacy here. God's breath, which was the final act of image making, caused his heart to beat, his blood to flow, and his lungs to breath. God's breath caused all Adam's senses to come alive. Adam stood up a man with God's own life in him. Men, you were created to be just who God designed you to be. Men are uniquely created different from women. This was the sovereign purpose of God. He made us purposely and uniquely different from all other living creatures. If men and women will embrace and except this it will lead to the fixing and setting right again all social and cultural ills. Even the ills of today. It won't be easy. It won't be without enormous struggle. Nevertheless, it must happen. Men, do you feel special? You ought to, because you are.

God already had Adam's life purpose designed before Adam was formed. This is why it's so important for God to be a man's first priority. We need to know God's plan for our lives. It's true, men, God had a plan and purpose for your life before you were even born. Jeremiah 29:11 says, [11] *"For I know the plans I have for you,"* says the LORD. *"They are plans for good and not for disaster, to give you a future and a hope."* God has a plan for you now in your present AND for your future. You will not reach a time when God says, "ok that's enough I'm done with you, you can retire now." The question that is loud in my head is DO YOU KNOW GOD'S PLAN FOR YOUR LIFE? You can, you should, you must! Men, I want you to feel special because you are special. You are the apple of God's eye. His first image bearer. It has taken me many years to see this. I'm so glad I do, and now I want to live the rest of my life being the man God designed me to be. I hope you will too.

CHAPTER 3

THE GOD MADE MAN PRIORITIZES GOD

All of us know how to prioritize. In every man's life there is priority. Consider the things that are important to you. People are important to you, your wife, children, and friends. The "quality" time spent with them shows their priority in your life, or it can reveal a lack of priority. Your hobbies are important to you. As a boy I grew up with a love for hunting, fishing, and golf. I still enjoy it, so I prioritize time for each. Those people and things we enjoy, we prioritize time for them. So, prioritizing time isn't new to us. Prioritizing the most important people, activities, and things in our life will require choice and discipline. It doesn't just happen. As we look further into Adam's life I want us to understand what it is to make God your number one priority. It is the first thing God established with Adam, therefore it must be the first priority with every man.

BIBLICAL PRINCIPLE: If it was priority for God and Adam then the same biblical principle apply to us.

GOD TEACHES ADAM PRIORITY

There Adam is a full-grown man standing there brand new in that new wonderful world. Imagine with me the first thoughts that went through his head. Imagine the first sights he saw. Imagine the first sounds he heard, imagine his first smells, and he was not afraid. Oh, how wonderfully special that was. God made Adam for God with God's life and purpose breathed into him. Then God does something that we'll look at next. He spends time with him, lots of time. I want you to consider this question as you think of God spending time with Adam. How much time did He spend with Adam? We will examine the answer to this question and how it relates to us today as we look further into Genesis 2 because it's key to understanding God being your first priority.

It is with Adam, (man) that God chose to spend time with FIRST. We see no where in Genesis 1-3 God spending time with Eve this way. Was God showing that He favored men over women? Of course not. But understanding this for yourself is important. God was establishing order and priority when He created Adam first and spent this incredible amount of time with him. In this I want all men to see just how important you are as a man to God.

Notice what God does next in Genesis 2. Verse 8 says, *"Then the LORD God planted a garden in Eden in the*

east, and there he placed the man he had made." In understanding your importance to God I want you to see the
time God spent with Adam, and Adam with God. As
you read this it's my hope you will see your importance
to God even now in your life. When your relationship
with God is your first priority you will understand the
power of time spent with Him. The Bible says *"Then
God planted a garden in Eden and there He placed the man."*
This garden was not made for God, it was made for
Adam. Only Adam and no one else at this time. Men,
this is how special and important you are to God. No
matter your age, no matter where you exist, no matter
your current circumstances, God wants to gather you to
Himself and show you your importance to Him. God
knows who you are and where you are and how you
got there. He knows all of your life, the good and the
bad. Men, we stand in a long line of men down through
the ages who have failed. From Adam until now, the list
is long. Your failures will not keep God from using you.
And NOW God wants you to see His plan for you. God
placed Adam where He wanted him to be and then He
began to spend time with him showing him His
purpose for his life. Look what it says again. The Bible
says God "placed him" in the garden. It's vitally important that you understand how involved God must be in
"placing you" in your life, relationships, and your vocation. My dear brother, now is your time. It is never too
late to get on board with God.

Then the Bible says in Genesis 2:9,15, [9] *"The LORD
God made all sorts of trees grow up from the ground, trees
that were beautiful and that produced delicious fruit. In the*

middle of the garden he placed the tree of life and the tree of
the knowledge of good and evil. [15] The LORD God placed
the man in the Garden of Eden to tend and watch over it."
God made all the beautiful fruit producing trees and the
tree of life and the tree of knowledge of good and evil.
And there He placed Adam to "tend and watch over it."

ADAM DIDN'T HAVE TO FIGURE OUT WHAT HIS PURPOSE IN LIFE WAS

The first thing we see as God's plan for Adam is to
care for the garden. God made it clear for Adam what
his purpose in life was. God didn't place him there and
walk away and say, "now Adam, you figure out the
rest, if you need me I'll be around." Adam knew
because God "placed him" and showed him. Here's the
biblical principle for us today. When you prioritize God,
you will know God's plan for your life. God's plans for
Adam were only beginning to be revealed. Too many
men go through life never knowing their purpose.
Brothers, God didn't form you to not know. He already
has your purpose fixed, but you must seek Him so He
can show you. John Eldridge says in his book "Wild At
Heart," "Adam was the first and most brilliant horticulturalist." Get this, men; Adam did not choose his vocation, God did. This was part of his vocation and God
was his teacher. Adam was made for this. Adam wasn't
left to figure it out for himself. God chose his vocation
for him. Do you want to know what God's plan is for
your life? Then seek Him, draw near to Him, spend
time with Him. He will show you.

We never read where Adam says, "I don't know God, I don't think I can do this." God created Adam for this important purpose in the garden. Just as Adam was "created" for his life purpose (and because you're a man,) YOU were created for yours. If we decide to start spending the necessary time with God seeking His will for our lives it may surprise most of us what He says. Too many of us are floundering like fish in trees and squirrels in water because we are not living the life God has designed for us.

I knew from the age of 14 that God wanted me to preach. I'll never forget that night in a revival meeting when God began to impress on me that He was calling me to preach. I was scared to death. I knew it was God. I felt like I was the only one in the church building. It was me and God and He was loud and clear in my young heart. I said *yes* and my life's course was set. I now look back on my life and thank God for His choice to use me. It has not always been easy. There have been many challenges. Many difficult times; some because of my own selfish choices. Some of the difficulties were simply part of the growing processes. But I have seen God do amazing things in my life and in the lives of others because I said yes to God. Now I'm on a new path designed by God and I am so excited for the future. Men, there's nothing better than being in "the garden" that God has prepared you for.

HOW MUCH TIME DID GOD AND ADAM SPEND TOGETHER BEFORE EVE?

Like I said before, this is where we miss it as men, women as well. We know that God is supposed to be our number one priority but too often we jump into trying to figure out how to deal with our other priorities like relationships, home life, others, and vocation without nailing down priority number one which is God and you. I want this to be your never-ending pressing question, "how much time is the right amount of time?" The answer is, when the balance is right, you'll know. Here's what I can tell you, your home life, your relationship with others, and your relationship with your vocation will be healthy. Not without challenges but healthy.

Let's further examine God and Adam's time together. As we've already seen, Adam was a master horticulturalist because God made him that way. Imagine the many different species of tree and plant life, and the time God spent with Adam teaching him about them and the garden. God was his teacher and He taught him how to care for the garden. This took much time.

Now let's look at the next responsibility God gave Adam and the time God and Adam spent together. In Genesis 2:18-20 it says, *[18] Then the LORD God said, "It is not good for the man to be alone. I will make a helper who is just right for him." (What makes Adam's helper just right for him? He's helped. The helper helps him.) [19] So the LORD God formed from the ground all the wild animals and all the birds of the sky. He brought them to the man to see what he would call them, and the man chose a name for each one. [20] He gave names to all the livestock, all the birds of the sky, and all the wild animals. But still there was no helper just right for him."*

I have to admit, this is one of those passages I've read and known all my life. To me it was simply part of the creation story. I never thought about it in any other way. But ever since my friend's sermon on God's sovereignty when he made that statement about Genesis 1,2, and 3 being the foundation to it all, I now understand what prioritizing God with your time will do.

If you're like me you've read Genesis 2:18-20 and thought, "ok so Adam named the animals, let's move on." But wait, stop and look carefully at this. This is where I hope you'll appreciate my repeated emphasis on time spent with God. I ask you to consider this question. Not only were there thousands of species of plant and tree life, how many species of birds and animals are there and how long did it take Adam to name them all? Thanks to today's technology and google, the number of species is a quick search. Turns out there are between 2.7 million and 8 million species of animals on the planet, so let's say 5 million. Genesis 2:18 says, *"He (God) brought them to the man to see what he would call them, and the man chose a name for **each** one."* This wasn't a rapid assembly line. God brought each species to Adam for him to know them and name them. Men, you need to see this, this was a joint effort between God and Adam. Adam named 5 million species of animals and birds. How long do you think this took, months, years? I don't know, but I can say this with certainty, it took a

LONG time. When I stop and think about this I laugh. There Adam is counting, naming, and learning about each species then about the 3 millionth animal God brings, this strange looking species with an odd shaped hairy body, claws for digging, a long snout, and an even longer tongue. Adam looks at it and says, "Oh heck, God, I don't know, Aardvark. Next!" It didn't happen that way but as we can see, God and Adam spent a lot of time together. God teaching Adam, Adam learning about each species, and Adam learning from God. Men, this is why I say that if you're going to make God first in your life it requires focused time. Time to hear from God, time to listen and learn, time to understand, and time to grow in trust and love with Him.

Again, John Eldredge says, "So not only did God make Adam a master horticulturalist, He made him a biologist focusing on zoology and the study of animals." God did this with and for Adam. He created him for this purpose. Men, much will come from you spending time with God. From this we see another biblical principle, that God will show you your purpose in your life's vocation. Go ahead, ask yourself, will God really show me what to do in life? Clearly the answer is YES! Some of you have dreams that you've tucked away and are now deep within your hearts. Could these dreams actually be what God created you to be and do? Go ahead and spend time with God and see what He says.

Remember what I said earlier that God called me to preach when I was 14 years old? After I married I took a job as an electricians apprentice. It made since because my dad was a master electrician and I had worked with him during summers. But I was like a fish in a tree. Then I worked at Cooper Tire and Rubber Company in Texarkana working different jobs finally becoming a tire builder for 9 years, but again I was a squirrel in water. I wasn't fulfilled. But then, I started spending focused time with God and seeking Him and He led me to enroll in Seminary taking Bible classes and it was then I began to really hear God's voice. It wasn't long after that God led me to my first church to pastor in 1982. I was finally doing what God created me to do, preaching and teaching the word of God helping people grow as Christians and reaching the lost. It all happened because I seriously started seeking His will and purpose for my life like never before. It can happen for you. It MUST happen for you. Men, your culture and the people in your life depend on you knowing God's plan for your life.

Priority number one is men spending time with God seeking Him, listening to Him, and learning from Him. Start by asking yourself, "am I spending the time with God that God requires of me? Is there something better that God has for me?" You are a man. Your whole life and everyone in your life is depending on it.

Before we go further let me help you understand "time spent with God." Notice that we never see Adam in a quiet corner of the garden with his Bible and journal, and praying. The Bible, journal, and prayer is usually how we understand spending time with God. The Bible hadn't been written yet and there were no journals. Adam lived his daily life with God. As he worked the garden and tended the animals, he did it with God. Men, we as Christians today need to learn how to have a daily relationship with God as we go through our days. Like Adam, you can walk with God at home, work, on the lake, in the woods, on your horse, in the arena, on the golf course, in your home, wherever. It's a lifestyle. There are times that a man needs to get alone with God, his Bible, and prayer, but your prayer closet is not the only place and time we spend with God. My dad was not a "prayer closet" kind of father. To him, it was a lifestyle. He lived it at home, on his job, and among his family and friends. It's the reason he was so admired by those who knew him.

Now look what God does next with Adam. He creates Eve and brings her to him, but not until He and Adam have completed their time together. Not until God had an established relationship with Adam. Eve wasn't introduced to Adam until God decided it was time. Those months and years weren't Eve's time, it was Adam's time with God. One of the biggest reasons marriages fail today is because men don't know who they are as men created by God. And, the second reason is that men fail to do what God created them to do. Men, you need to be ready for your Eve. An important part of being ready for your Eve is knowing who God made you to be and what He made you to do.

CHAPTER 4

THE GOD MADE MAN IS READY FOR HIS EVE

After the long process of God and Adam naming the animals and God establishing Adam, it is then He creates Eve. Look carefully at this. Men, I invite you to open your heart to the biblical truths and principles here. This may challenge what you've believed. It may even be teaching you've never heard before. I can promise you this, today's progressive woman will strongly disagree with this. Anti-cultural truth is often hard to embrace but we must! The details in these verses have gone overlooked by men and women for too long. They were certainly overlooked by me. After many years I now see this and I'm so glad I do. In Genesis 2:20-22 it says, *[20] He gave names to all the livestock, all the birds of the sky, and all the wild animals. But still there was no helper just right for him. [21] So the LORD God caused the man to fall into a deep sleep. While the man slept, the LORD God took out one of the man's ribs and* *closed up the opening. [22] Then the LORD God **made** a woman from the rib, and he brought her to the man."*

Men, this is packed full of important biblical truths (principles) I want you to prayerfully consider. ONE, Genesis 2:20 says, *"still there was no helper just right for him."* Keep in mind, God is still focused on Adam, making him the man He wants him to be. I say this because the heart of God has not changed for men. It is we men who must realign with God's plan. *"Just right"* are God's words about Adam, not Moses's. It's what God wants Adam to experience. Do you understand what that "just right" thing is for men? It's a "knowing," there's "no doubt," it's when everything is "clicking." Athletes call it being in the "zone." I was an avid runner in my 50s and for me it was "hitting my stride." I could be 13 miles into a marathon and it was almost effortless. Notice I said *almost*. Because you're a man, God has a plan for things in your life to be "just right." Even in the up and down world you live in, you can experience life in the "just right zone." But doing life God's way and being the man God created you to be is the key. Let's go deeper.

TWO, as we read Genesis 2:20 we clearly see God's focus is still on Adam. Here are some questions to consider. God uses the word "helper." What did Adam need help with? The word "helper" here means one who aids and assists. As we look deeper into that question we need to understand that God created Adam with the same human need all men have, a need for help. In other words, there will be times when help from others is what will be needed for the man to be at his best. For me a good way to understand "helper" is explained like this. Every man knows what a sawhorse is. By itself it's strong enough to support the weight of the work but alone it's not fully effective. But when you add the second sawhorse to the job more weight is supported, you can make longer straighter cuts, therefore the work is made easier. For some things in life it takes two. Ecclesiastes 4:9-12 says it this way, *[9] Two are better than one, because they have a good reward for their toil. [10] For if they fall, one will lift up his fellow. But woe to him who is alone when he falls and has not another to lift him up! [11] Again, if two lie together, they keep warm, but how can one keep warm alone? [12] And though a man might prevail against one who is alone, two will withstand him, a threefold cord is not quickly broken."* Those men who say, "I'm self made, I don't need anyone else" are setting themselves up for failure. As a man you were created by God to need help. He designed you that way. Not that we're lacking something as a man. We're not! We are complete but part of our completeness is a need to be helped in life. God has put a plan in place to make us better men. When the need for help that's in us is met, we become the men God created us to be, His image bearer. God worked in cooperation with his son and Jesus worked in cooperation with his Father. Jesus worked with the disciples and they worked with Him. Our need for help makes relationships necessary in our lives. God never intended for Adam to be alone but the animals couldn't meet his need.

Remember what Genesis 2:18 says, *"It is not good for the man to be alone."* No, God did not miscalculate when

He put that space of "need for help" in Adam, (in a man). It was to help him be the best he could be. So I say again to all you "self made men," Mr. Man, you weren't made to do your life alone. The sooner we understand and embrace this the sooner we'll be the men God made us to be.

THREE, the third biblical principle I want you to consider is in verse [21], it says, *"So the LORD God caused the man to fall into a deep sleep."* This is important to see. God could've made Eve the same way He made Adam, from a clump of moist dust, dirt, and clay, but He didn't. She was made differently and here's the biggest difference. The making of woman (Eve) did not happen without Adam. Why? It was God's sovereign choice to do it this way for the purpose of setting in motion God's foundational fundamentals for the husband and wife relationship. It is in these next few verses that I pray your eyes will be opened to God's amazing fundamental truths about men and women. To know how to be a God Made Man you must understand this.

Look at the care God gives in this surgical process. God was just as careful, intimate, and meticulous with the creation of Eve as He was with Adam. But very different. Men, you've got to see this. God took no short cuts with Eve. It is with great care that he creates the man and woman relationship because God is making a helper for Adam. God completes Adam by making Eve. I believe there was a conversation between God and Adam as He explained to Adam what was about to happen. The Bible doesn't say that but what it does say leads me to believe the following. We read, *"So the LORD God caused the man to fall into a deep sleep."* Notice Moses writes "so the LORD God <u>caused</u>." It is God the Father, God of heaven and all creation doing the creating here with his own hands. Four of our most popular Bible translations say "caused." In my mind, I see God taking a prepared Adam into His hands and carefully laying him down. The word "caused" tells me an action was taken that placed Adam into a deep sleep. This was not a rush job. God understood what He was creating. He understood the social, cultural, and world implications. There had never been a woman on earth before. She will be brand new to the garden culture. But most importantly He understood what He was doing for Adam. He was further blessing Adam and in this process making him a better man. Ladies, did you hear that? Do you hear how important you are in God's created plan? God was making a helper for Adam who would be able to fill his space of loneliness and "need for help" that the animals couldn't do. This caused action, this surgery, this making of Eve was for Adam, God's first and most important image bearer. Adam was the one He told everything to about the garden, the tree of knowledge and good and evil. He taught him about the tree of life. Adam was the one who God taught about the trees and plants and the animal kingdom. For a long time God spoke with Adam sharing all things, building a relationship with him. All that Adam learned from God, Adam would now share and teach to Eve. Listen to this men and ladies. The Bible does not mention that God spoke to Eve until after she sinned in

Genesis 3. It was Adam's responsibility to share, teach, and lead Eve and in doing so build a loving relationship with her just as God did with Adam. As Adam submitted to God so God could teach him, Eve was created to submit to Adam so he could teach her. The apostle Paul later paints this picture in a way we can better understand it when he wrote in Ephesians 5:22-24 NLT,*[22] For wives, this means submit to your husbands as to the Lord. [23] For a husband is the head of his wife as Christ is the head of the church. He is the Savior of his body, the church. [24] As the church submits to Christ, so you wives should submit to your husbands in everything.*

So there he is now in a deep sleep before surgery. If you've ever undergone surgery you understand this. We are all happy for the deep sleep. The doctor explains what you are about to feel and the next thing you know you're waking up in recovery. It's a good thing that Adam was put in a deep sleep. God was about to perform major surgery with His own hands. His own hands! To me, that is just mind-blowingly special. God began the human race being physically intimate with them and now through Jesus and the cross the intimacy with God the Father continues.

The fourth biblical principle is this, the Bible says, *"While the man slept, the LORD God took out one of the man's ribs and closed up the opening."* When Adam says later she is "bone of my bone and flesh of my flesh" he's making a literal factual statement. Adam was aware of how the rest of creation was made but he knew Eve was exclusively and profoundly made differently. God opened Adam's side and removed one of his ribs covered with sinew, wrapped with muscle and dripping in Adam's blood. But there's more. Listen to this; the bone, blood, and flesh of Adam had the very life of God He had earlier breathed into it. It wasn't just a hunk of flesh and bone. It held God's very life in it. God and Adam were connected, just as we are connected to God through Jesus, because divine nature and life was breathed into him. It was Adam that possessed God's life-giving breath. It was Adam that experienced relationship with God before Eve. This will be significantly important later, men, so don't forget this.

Adam and Eve were created in two very different ways for two very different reasons. *[22] "Then the LORD God **made** a woman from the rib, and he brought her to the man."* As we've seen earlier Adam was "formed" as a potter would form clay into a useable vessel. Eve was not formed. A very different word is used to describe her creation. She was "made." This next part is going to be controversial. It will be truthful, it will be biblical, but it is going to fly in the face of what has become our social norms. Men, we must understand what God's intentions were when He made Eve and every woman after her must understand the same.

GOD'S TRUTH IS OUR PLUMB LINE

In ancient Egypt a measuring device was developed for determining the vertical straightness of a structure, the plumb-line. The plumb-line is a string with a heavy object on the end usually a stone or piece of metal with a point on it. When the plumb-line was lowered next to a building being constructed you could see with your eye if the structure was perfectly straight or slightly off center.

God's word is our plumb-line and when it is dropped into our lives, we must except what it shows us. The truths we find in the way God created Adam and Eve were meant for every man and woman after them. The centuries and changing cultures haven't altered this truth. Let's see now what God originally did and what it means for us today.

Verse 22 says, *"Then the LORD God **made** a woman from the rib, and he brought her to the man."* Let's slow down here and allow ourselves to look at Eve's creation with the same attention we did Adam's. God now has in His hands Adam's rib dripping in blood wrapped with muscle and sinew. God has in His mind every physical, emotional, mental, and relational detail about Eve. Then God does something He didn't do with Adam. He "made" her. The biblical word "made" here is a construction term. A contractor builds, erects, and constructs things, a potter forms and shapes things. Why did God create them using two different methods? I think the answer is to establish a clear difference between Adam and Eve, man and woman. Even the way they were created God chose to do differently. Even though they have some of the same physical abilities they are very different. Adam has the mind of a man, Eve has the mind of a woman. They were created to process thoughts from a different perspective. Look at their bodies. They both have ten fingers, ten toes, two eyes, and two ears. But, there are some very clear and special differences that only a woman and a man have. And God designed their body features for specific reasons of which one is our mutual pleasure, and the other is procreation. These body features set us apart with distinction. We both have distinctive reproductive abilities but Eve was made very differently. Eve was made to have sex with Adam, receive his seed and give birth to other humans. Therefore, every woman after her is made the same way.

In this day of "confusion" about sexual orientation and identity which is the result of Satan's lies and human layering, with God it wasn't confusing. He clearly created a vivid distinction. There is a man and a woman period! I for one am happy happy happy for the differences. As a man I love our differences. No other created thing does to and for a man what a woman can do. And Adam immediately saw with his eyes their differences. Not only did he know she was made from his very own flesh and bone, Eve stirred something in him no other created thing before her could do, and he spent a long time with God's creation. Can I get a hallelujah and amen?

Let's consider for a moment some other obvious differences. Some that the Bible doesn't mention but are clearly present. Even though, like Adam she was created as a young adult, she had not yet experienced the complexities of a man nor the beauty and vastness of the garden. She didn't have the horticultural knowledge and skills Adam was given. She didn't have the knowledge of the animal kingdom Adam was given. Think about it. Adam knew how to care for every kind of tree and plant life in the garden. He knew how to cultivate the ground of the garden. Adam knew the names and nature of five million species of animals on the planet. And listen, God did not teach Eve these things because it was Adam's responsibility to share this with her. It was God who taught Adam and it was Adam's responsibility to teach Eve. Do you hear and see the biblical balance of the husband and wife relationship in this? Eve was to learn from a strong, courageous, godly man as he leads her. This hasn't changed. It's a biblical principle for today.

THEIR ONE FLESH RELATIONSHIP

So, there she is made, complete, and alive, the second image bearer. But there's one huge difference in how God created Eve. And this difference binds Adam and Eve together. The Bible calls it "one flesh." This is far more than a physical sexual binding. Eve needed Adam. She was literally part of him. God created her to need and depend on him. Let me explain. But before I do, I want to address the number one biggest difference between Adam and Eve's creation. I spoke to it earlier. Warning, this is where the proverbial "crap will hit the fan" with many today. The Bible says, *"Then the LORD God made a woman from the rib, and he brought her to the man."* Do you see it? Do you see what's not said about Eve that God did exclusively to Adam? This is a central truth for fully understanding the relationship dynamic between Adam, Eve, and God, husband, wife, and God. It helps us understand why Eve needed her husband. In

Genesis 2:7 it says, *"Then the LORD God formed the man from the dust of the ground. He **breathed** the breath of life into the man's nostrils, and the man became a living person."* This verse tells us specifically how Adam became a living person. God breathed His breath of life into Adam's nostrils and by this, God gave Adam His own life. This one physical act made Adam dependent on God. It bound Adam to God. It completed the "image making" process. I believe Adam knew from their many conversations the origin of his life.

Now do you see the major difference between Adam's coming to life and Eve's? The Bible records that only Adam received God's breath of life. No other created living thing, not even Eve received this. So here it is, men, just as God's life giving breath bound Adam to God, that same life was in the rib-bone, sinew, muscle and blood that God removed from Adam and made Eve. God's life, His image, was in that bone and flesh. Eve was connected to God through Adam by the way God constructed her. She is now "made in God's image" through Adam's bone flesh and blood. Her greatest need was a "one flesh" relationship with her husband as Adam's was with God. Her life, her existence depended on God through Adam. Her survival depended on God through Adam. Her identity and self worth was connected to God through Adam. Are you seeing where I'm going with this? Eve's own understanding and knowledge of God, His ways, what He commanded, all that He said and taught Adam about the garden and the animals, right and wrong, tree of life and tree of knowledge of good and evil, EVERYTHING, would be taught her by her husband. <u>Eve was connected to God through her husband</u>. The order is, God-husband-wife-children-vocation. Priority order number one must be, God-Adam, God-husband. Stop for a moment and think about this before reading on!

This same biblical principle is for the husband and wife relationship today. The time that Adam and God spent together caused Adam's love for God to grow and deepen which was the purpose for time spent with God. Theirs was a true Father and earthly son relationship. This is what God intended by spending all that time with Adam. In doing so, God taught Adam how to grow a loving relationship with another human, his wife.

When the Bible says in verse 22, *"and <u>he brought her to the man,"</u>* God does exactly what he does with each of the animals. He brings them to Adam to name them, spend time with each one getting to know each species. Now, God does the same with Eve, He brings her to Adam. I can't emphasize the power of the husband and wife connection enough. Young men hear this. As you build your relationship with God, at the right time, He will bring you your Eve. Adam immediately recognizes the difference in Eve from all other living things on earth. He sees that she's like him, a human and co-image bearer, he understands their physical connection and the implications, and then he identifies her and calls her "woman" (v.23).

. . .

WHAT MORE CAN WE LEARN ABOUT MEN AND WOMEN

Let's examine this further and see what more we can learn about men and women today. I believe there are biblical principles for us all in what we see God doing with Adam and Eve. I hope you will allow yourself to see it as well. What are these principles?

One, God clearly made two, only two separate genders. If you are a man with a man or a woman with a woman you are living in sin and outside of God's original created plan. If you are confused about your gender, if you're part of the LGBTQ+ plus group today you are in sin and living outside God's plan for your life. This has not changed because God hasn't changed! I know the culture we live in has layered it differently but the truth and salvation of today's culture is found in what God originally said in the beginning. I know that directly goes against our current culture but it's absolute biblical truth. And that's what I'm calling all men back to.

Two, God is a God of order. He hasn't changed so He intends for there to be His order and His structure in every marriage. I'm only speaking of the arena of marriage. I'm not speaking of the secular world where women can hold positions of authority over men. But, in God's plan, Adam was first and when Adam was ready God made Eve from the bone, flesh, and blood of Adam that had God's life in it. The fact that Adam was the first image bearer and Eve was the second doesn't mean she was less important. She is vitally important in the role God made her for. Eve was the fulfillment of

God's plan for Adam, therefore God's plan for her. Man and woman are of equal importance in God's plan.

Three, God then brings the living woman to Adam. God joins them. There's God, Adam, and Eve as it must be. There was no doubt with either of them that they were created for each other. This act of God bringing her to Adam was firstly for Adam and secondly for Eve. Eve's life and existence depended on this connection. As I said earlier Eve needs Adam. Adam now must learn everything about Eve as he did with all the plant life and animals. This would take time. He now must teach and share with her all God has said about life in the garden, the trees, plants, and the animals, and God's instructions. This would take time. As a result, a deep love would grow between them as it did with God and Adam. This was God's will and is God's will for husbands and wives today.

Four, here's the big one, and yes I know it's going to be controversial but it must be said and we must bring our understanding of marriage back into alignment with God's will and biblical principles. Eve needed her husband. Her life and connection to God came through Adam. Her identity, "woman" was given to her by Adam. Her significance and self worth from God is experienced in her relationship with Adam. Her relationship with God was experienced through Adam. Wives were designed by God to need their husbands just as men were designed by God to need their wives. Men, if you're wanting to high-five and chest bump each other remember this, wives are designed to be led by strong confident loving husbands who are godly biblical men. That's the kind of man Adam was to Eve. Wives need their husbands to lead, guide, and protect them. When a husband does this and when a wife submits to this, real love, real joy, real happiness, and real fulfillment will be experienced. I feel this needs to be said here, I'm talking about life and relationship before "the fall." These original principles need to be filtered through the leadership of the Holy Spirit in our marriages today.

For some reason we've come to believe that since we've been saved and filled with the Holy Spirit that we are now individually independent. Yes, we each have the Holy Spirit and we are each responsible to Him, but the husband and wife were created for each other to be one flesh in accordance to God's creation order.

This hasn't changed because God hasn't changed, but sadly we have adopted unbiblical changes that our culture now says is a better way. When a society embraces standards that are opposite of biblical teachings you have what we have today, the destruction of the traditional home and marriage, the emasculation of men, the elevation of women over men they were not designed for, loss of respect for authority, the homosexual lifestyle is accepted as normal, LGBTQ+ plus gender confusion is created, and traditional common sense Christian values are swallowed up by the leftist progressive feckless agenda. The answer is still found in God's word. Men, we must be the authentic man God made us to be. Women, you must be the authentic woman God made you to be, and those truths are found in Genesis 1,2,&3.

Before we move on to the next chapter I want to state the obvious. When you drop the plumb line of God's word into today's world culture it clearly reveals that not only has culture shifted, it has collapsed. This is why it's so important for men to return to God's word and erase the layers of our wrong beliefs. We must go back to the beginning again as Jesus challenges us to do, and as one man and one woman, put God and His order for our lives first. Men, it must begin with you.

CHAPTER 5

HOW QUICKLY THE GOOD LIFE CAN BE LOST

Genesis 3 reveals much about what a man and a woman are prone to do when it comes to difficult decision making. This chapter gives us a vivid look into the tendencies of both and therefore a glimpse into our own tendencies today. Remember, these were the first created humans, created by God. I think it's safe to say that what we see in God's first humans is a look into every man and woman after them. We are going to look carefully at their behaviors. We'll ask why they did or didn't do some things and talk about possible answers that I hope will shed some light on why we as men and women are prone to behave the way we do today.

This has been a personal journey for me. As I said earlier, I've been taking a hard close look at myself through the scriptural microscope of Genesis 1-3. It has been an eye opening experience into myself that I've desperately needed. I'm thankful for what God is teaching me and I'm looking forward to sharing it with you.

THEIRS WAS HEAVEN ON EARTH

The last verse in Genesis 2 says, [25] *Now the man and his wife were both naked, but they felt no shame."* For Adam and Eve life was good! You and I have never lived and experienced what they did. It was as though God fired His starting pistol after all was created and off they went living the real good life. Theirs was heaven on earth, no sin, no shame, no suffering, and no fear. It was true paradise and God was their constant companion. They were living in complete harmony with God and each other as God created them to be. It was life on earth as God intended. Again, the question "how long" before the fall did they live in peace and harmony together pops into my mind. No one can say for sure but it was time enough for Adam to teach and show everything to Eve about the garden, plant and tree life, and the animal kingdom. And in spending such time together a pure love relationship grew between them both. Do you remember those early weeks and months between you and your sweetheart? When two people, who are made for each other, spend time learning each other, they grow deeper in love.

But know this, what God had established in creation, Satan was already plotting and strategizing a way to destroy. You must remember Evil wasn't new. Satan had already been in existence. He watched the whole creation event happen and heard everything God told Adam.

In Genesis 3 we find the story of the human fall into sin. We also learn even more about the nature of a man and the nature of a woman. What we'll learn from Eve's encounter with Satan will reveal what I believe are every woman's greatest tendencies and weaknesses. What we'll learn from Adam's behavior and fall will reveal what I believe are every man's greatest tendencies and weaknesses. It is good that we look at this and learn these biblical principles which are meant for all men and women today. These lessons must be learned by all of us. I challenge you not to fall into Satan's trap and say, "O that's not who I am." These are the weaknesses and tendencies in every single man and woman. After Adam and Eve's sin, we are born into sin and a sinful world. Therefore, if it was in Adam and Eve, God's first humans, it's in us.

A personal plea to both. Men, read and listen carefully. There is biblical truth about yourself and the nature of women that ALL men must understand. Ladies, read and listen carefully. There is biblical truth about yourself and the nature of men that ALL women must understand. As we did in the creation story we are going to go deep in the story of the fall of Adam and Eve. There is much that God is saying here that every man must see and understand. Again I will share some of my own life experiences, failures and successes in hopes that a little of my story may help and encourage you. I'm just one man on this rock called earth who is extremely thankful for all I've experienced and am learning.

THE FALL OF MAN WAS <u>SHREWDLY</u> PLANNED

Before we dig into this, let's take a step back and get a broader look at what's about to happen. This moment didn't catch God off guard. He knew what was about to happen and He knew how, the time, day, and place it would happen. Our sovereign God is sovereign over all time and events in our lives. Some may ask, "if God's a loving God why didn't God stop Adam and Eve from eating the fruit?" That's a good and common question people often ask when life takes a bad turn. It's important to remember that God already gave them His boundaries. So, with His commands and instructions He *did* stop this from happening, but they would have to do their part. Obey! God had already told them what they could and couldn't do. God's commands were their "prevention" to keep this from happening. For instance, Exodus 20:15 says, *"You shall not steal."* Yet people steal anyway. By giving the command "not to steal," by giving the command to Adam and Eve "not to eat the fruit" this is God giving boundaries that if we live within them we won't disobey God. In Genesis 4:7 God says this to Cain before he murders his brother Able, *"If you do well, will you not be accepted? And if you do not do well, sin is crouching at the door. It's desire is contrary to you, but you must rule over it."* Adam and Eve were prepared with God's truth for what was about to happen. God's truth is a boundary around us all. The

New Testament says in James 4:17 *"So whoever knows the right thing to do and fails to do it, for him it is sin."* Adam and Eve, like us, will have a choice to make. What will they choose?

ENTER THE SERPENT

Genesis 3 begins with the serpent, *"The serpent was the shrewdest of all the wild animals the LORD God had made."*

The word "shrewd" is important for us to understand about the devil. Men, you will never outwit, out-calculate, or out-smart the devil. He is the master of deception and manipulation. Eve, and Adam, will learn this in a tragic way.

According to scripture, spiritual warfare is a constant part of the Christian life. You need a singular dependence on God, Jesus, and the Holy Spirit. And, you need others. Satan shrewdly waited for the most opportune moment to advance on Eve. She was probably near or next to the tree of knowledge of good and evil and she was alone without her husband. That's important to understand, I'll explain shortly.

Moses, who authored the book of Genesis, introduces Satan in the form of a serpent. Notice where he is, in the perfect God-made garden. Men, never forget this, Satan is going to be in and around your world the rest of your life. We live in His world. Don't let this discourage you. Encounters with him are opportunities for victories. And every battle, failure, and victory makes us wiser and stronger. We have a great promise from Jesus. Even though we live in a fallen world Jesus said in John 16:33, *"I have told you all this so that you may have peace in me. Here on earth you will have many trials and sorrows. But take heart, because I have overcome the world."*

SATAN'S SHREWD ADVANCE

So there the devil is shrewdly making his way to Eve, the Bible says, *"One day he asked the woman, 'Did God really say you must not eat the fruit from any of the trees in the garden?"* [Genesis 3:1]. I have heard and read many times the statement I'm about to say and I remember the impact it made on my life. Men, notice who Satan approaches. It's Eve, Adam's wife. Make no mistake here, Satan's primary target is not Eve. It is Adam the husband and ultimately God and all that God had said and established with Adam. Satan has hated God and men from the beginning. He knows if he can destroy authentic manhood he can destroy everything. Look around, there are men all around us who hold important leadership positions in government, business, religion, and life today who are weak, feckless, lying weenies relying on others to tell them what to do. In every generation this has been so. Oh, don't be unaware, he hates women too. But Satan sees a strong Holy God and a strong godly authentic man as his biggest threat because he knows God's created order and purpose. Ask yourself, "If Adam was his primary target then why didn't he attack him?" The answer is clear. It was Adam who had walked with God for a long time, possibly several years. He had the experiential one on one relationship with God. They were tight! As we'll see in Genesis 3, Eve knew what God had said because Adam had taught her. But it was Adam who had the relationship with God directly and Eve's relationship with God was through Adam because she was made from him. I'll say again, *a godly authentic woman is designed by God to be dependent on a godly authentic man.* I know this goes upstream against what our culture believes and teaches. But what matters more, what God says in His written word or what culture says? I'll go with God!

THE SERPENT FOUND EVE ALONE

So Satan approaches Eve with a question. Now here's my personal belief. Some will disagree and that's ok. We know later in Genesis 3 that Adam was with Eve while she was engaged in this conversation with the serpent, but I don't believe he was with her in the beginning of their encounter. Here's why I believe this. Adam was in a loving relationship with Eve that grew from the time they spent together. A strong godly man's protective instincts are always just under the surface. And, when you have a tight relationship with God as Adam did you are more able to recognize the tactics of the enemy. I believe Satan shrewdly sought and waited for the right time, and found her alone. If Adam had been there in the beginning, I believe he would've done the strong man thing and shielded his wife. So why didn't Adam step in later and rescue her? The answer to this question is going to reveal one of the biggest weak-nesses of all men. I'll share it soon.

Genesis 3:1-2 says this about Eve's and the serpents encounter, [1] *"... One day he asked the woman, Did God really say you must not eat the fruit from <u>any</u> of the trees in the garden?" [2] Of course we may eat fruit from the trees in the garden,"* the woman replied."

Men, I want to give you my insights and what I believe God is teaching us. The Bible not only speaks clearly about men, but women as well. Part of learning about being a strong authentic man in a relationship with your wife is understanding what God is teaching about women. This encounter between Eve and the serpent raises very important questions that I want to discuss. One, why didn't Eve leave the serpent and find Adam when he started talking to her? The Bible gives no indication up to this point that animals could verbally communicate so I would think this would be startling to her. Two, again I ask, why didn't she leave and go get her husband? All we have is what Moses tells us. She heard what the serpent said and knew it was incorrect because her husband had told her the correct version. At this point she still has the opportu-nity to walk away and leave to the safety of her husband but she chooses not to. Throughout this tragic encounter Eve and Adam made many wrong and misguided choices which led to the fall. And it's in these choices that we learn about the tendencies of men and women.

Back to Eve, she engages with the serpent instead. For Eve, this is her "hold my beer moment." This is exactly what Satan wanted her to do. How did he do it? Remember, Satan knew Eve better than she knew herself. He knew that in her was a desire to correct, redirect, stand for herself, and control. He knew she would recognize what he said was incorrect. The serpent said *"...you must not eat of any trees in the garden."* Eve knew that was wrong so she corrects him, *"Of course we may eat fruit from the trees in the garden, the woman replied."* [3] *"It's only the fruit from the tree in the middle of the garden that we are not allowed to eat. God said, 'You must not eat it or even touch it; if you do, you will die.'"* Do you see it? Do you hear what Satan heard? Eve misquotes, adds to the words of God and the serpent heard her do it.

SATAN HAS HER WHERE HE WANTS HER

Eve is doing what is naturally in her to do, correcting, challenging, and attempting to control. The problem is, this isn't Eve's responsibility. God put Adam in charge of the garden before Eve was created. The garden and every living thing in it is Adam's responsibility. Nevertheless, she tells the serpent that he's wrong. I can't emphasize enough here; in the present spiritual and cultural climate of the garden it is Adam's responsibility to set things right. She tells the serpent what God did say, and then added something that God didn't say, yet she says God said it. She added, "or even touch it." Some believe Adam probably told Eve this so she would stay away from the tree. Maybe, but I don't believe that. I believe Adam was careful to tell Eve everything exactly as God told him because that would be the right thing for a loving, godly husband to do. God never told Adam not to touch the tree. The tree was in the middle of the garden that Adam was tasked by God to cultivate and care for. So touching the trees and plants would've been impossible to avoid and sometimes necessary. I believe Eve added "not to touch it" on her own. It's possible she just wanted to add her thoughts about it as she saw it. Never has what God said needed our adjustment or revision and never will, but Eve does just that. She is doing what the serpent did with God's words. The serpent added the word "any" which changed what was said about the trees. Eve did the same, she added words that God didn't say. So now she feels pretty confident about her position after correcting the serpent. There's a scene in John Wayne's movie "McLintock" when his wife played by Marine O'Hara chases down the buggy Wayne is riding away in. She catches it and jumps on the back of it and gives this "take that" smirk with the tilt of her head. That's how I see this scene between Eve and the serpent. I think Eve is feeling pretty good about herself for correcting Mr. serpent. But, like a spider that has wrapped its prey in a cocoon of web, she's trapped and doesn't know it.

Remember what I said earlier, we will learn the tendencies of men and women in the story of Adam and Eve. Eve should've left at the beginning, found Adam, told him what the serpent said and allowed her husband to handle this matter. But she's feeling confident in her abilities and handles it herself. Something needs to be said here. Eve possessed the ability to think and reason for herself. She was made in God's image, so of course she can. That's not the problem here. The problem is she chose to act and react outside of God's created order. It wasn't her place to engage with the serpent. It was her husband's. Now the serpent takes full advantage of his control over her. As Adam's wife, Eve needs Adam's oversight and protection. This encounter is proof of that. That's how God created them to be, but she steps into a role that wasn't hers.

I want to state again the obvious. God created women with a brain and the ability to think on their own. All humans have the ability to think and reason about any situation. God wants women to fully live using all their God given abilities. I personally like being in relationships with smart intelligent women with common sense. They don't intimidate me, they are a great help to me. Because Eve was made by God, He made her intellectually smart. She is HIS image bearer reflecting Him. Her intelligence and ability to think for herself is not the issue. Doing the right thing within God's created order is the issue. By engaging with the serpent she steps out of her role and steps into her husband's role. Living within God's created order is like living within an impenetrable boundary. We live under God's protection and His blessings.

Back to the serpent and Eve. The last thing recorded in Genesis 3:3 was *"if you do you will die."* This is something that was told Eve by her husband because God had said this to him. So the serpent, knowing he has Eve where he wants her, continues luring her to the destruction he has planned for Adam. He then said, *[4] "You won't die!" the serpent replied to the woman. [5] "God knows that your eyes will be opened as soon as you eat it, and you will be like God, knowing both good and evil."* Notice with me here, there's no reference about Adam. Moses's story still only includes Eve and the serpent. The serpent had just blatantly called God a liar by contradicting what He actually said. If Adam had arrived there at this time and heard this, I believe he would've stopped it because he knows God's not a liar.

Now, notice what the serpent says and how he says it, "You won't die, *Exclamation Point!*" He says it with strength, boldness, and authority. The way he said it got Eve's attention. Men, I want you to hear this; God made women to respond to the man's confidence, strength, boldness, and authority. Not mean, abusive, angry, and loud screams. Adam's responsibility was to teach and instruct Eve about everything God had said, and God made her to listen and respond accordingly because He wants her to know everything Adam knows. It's what made life so good between them in the garden. Adam was living as God created him, and Eve lived as God created her. But now, Eve is listening to the wrong authoritative voice and she is locked onto his words. He then starts massaging her female intellect. He says, *"God knows your eyes will be opened as soon as you eat it."* I believe she hears this and thinks, "Am I being prevented from seeing and knowing something?" Get this, she's listening to an absolute lie. He's looking her in the eye and lying to her and she's going along with it. She's now considering alternatives, a better way in her mind. Eve is listening to and now considering something she thinks is better for herself so therefore better for her husband. Each alternative belief different from her husband is a new layer of her own belief. Men, this is why it's imperative that we know God's will and word for our lives so that when other voices say something different, we'll remember what God says about us and reject the lie.

The serpent then says, *"and you will be like God, knowing both good and evil" [V5]*. He is in her head now. The Bible says in *James 1:14-15, [14] "Temptation comes from our own desires, which entice us and drag us away. [15] These desires give birth to sinful actions. And when sin is allowed to grow, it gives birth to death."* Eve knows who God is. She's heard and seen Him walking with Adam in the garden. She has been intimately part of their three way relationship. She knows God is good. She knows He's all powerful. She knows He knows everything. She's experienced His love and care for them both. So the tempter says, *"you will be like God, knowing both good and evil."* Here's what I believe she's thinking, "I'll know what God knows, everything. I'll even know more than my husband." Listen, God made Adam and Eve human with human tendencies and thought processes. They were created with the ability to reason and choose, therefore they could choose to sin. He knows what they were capable of because He made them. That's why He gave them clearly understood boundaries. He made it clear what they could and could not do. But Eve made a <u>choice</u> to follow a different voice. She listened to lies and untruths about

God, her husband's God, because the lies don't sound wrong to her now. Eve is not making a mistake or misstep. Sin is never a mistake, it's a human thought-out choice. Men, as we see in Eve, it is the tendency of women, their weakness, to look for a better way for themselves, their family, and their husband. Especially if they believe in their position over their husbands, as Eve now does. This is why our wives need a strong, godly, caring, loving, responsible leader in their lives to guide them as God guides us. One who puts God first and keeps him first in their lives.

I want to stress something here. As much as wives need their husbands, husbands need their wives. The wife and husband team is God's design. We were made for each other. We are two sawhorses. Each can stand on its own but there are many times life calls for two. And as the relationship grows, two are needed and wanted even more. God's a master designer.

EVE BELIEVES THE LIE

Then it happened. Eve believed the lies the serpent told her and she believed the lies she told herself. Therefore she believes what her husband told her was a lie and God must be holding out on her. Remember this men, Satan is a shrewd master manipulator. The Bible says in verse 6, *"The woman was convinced."* Personal belief is a powerful thing and when you're "convinced" in what you believe you will act on it.

Before we go to the next chapter, understand this is a tragic moment in this brand new period of human existence. The human history, which only included two humans in the very beginning, gets completely knocked off course by the manipulation of all our enemy. Eve was a woman made in the image of God. She was given all she needed by God. She's the smartest, most capable woman to ever live because of her creator. Yet, she's "convinced" to believe and do the opposite of what God has said. This is a forward look from the beginning into what the human race will be faced with. Therefore it is imperative that we men love God, keep Him first in our lives, and lead our wives and families as He leads us.

CHAPTER 6

THE GOD MADE MAN MUST NOT BE CAUGHT OFF GUARD

Men must be ready at all times to fight for their family. You never know when you will be called into battle to defend your wife and family against the enemy's attacks. As with Adam it will most likely happen when you least expect it. Adam was caught off guard. He wasn't expecting what he found.

Here's about the time when I believe Adam shows up. Somewhere around this time frame of Eve and the serpent's conversation after she's been deceived and now convinced, Adam walks up. Verse 6 is the first time Adam is mentioned in the encounter between Eve and the serpent. If he was with Eve in the beginning of the encounter between Eve and the serpent I believe Moses would've said so as he clearly mentioned the serpent and Eve.

So, Eve is now convinced. Convinced of what? She now sees a more better way for herself and her husband. So Adam walks up to his wife having a life altering conversation with this serpent. His wife is now believing something that's in absolute opposition to what he believes. She is in the complete control of Satan and a new way of thinking. The Bible says, *"She saw that the tree was beautiful and its fruit looked delicious, and she wanted the wisdom it would give her. So she took some of the fruit and ate it"* [V6]. Eve now sees the fruit of this tree not as something that's restricted by God as her husband had told her, but as something to embrace and receive. In her eyes now the tree is "beautiful" and the fruit "looks delicious." And God and her husband must be wrong. She sees a better way than what her husband told her. After being persuaded by Satan, she's now moving in her own understanding. Not the understanding given to her by her husband and God. The Bible then says, *"she wanted the wisdom it would give her"* [6]. It was the serpent that convinced her that what others had, God and Adam, she didn't have. He convinced her she was less than Adam. That Adam had something more and better than she had. Even more, for her to "be like God" would be a position not even her husband had. Yet here's the real truth, all that Adam is and has with God, Eve has because God made her from Adam. He put them together, and together they are one flesh. Because she's connected to Adam, she's connected to God. But she is now thinking only of herself. She's putting her wants, desires, dreams, and perceived needs ahead of everything, her husband, and God. Her new beliefs are her new layers, and she's convinced she's right. Pay close attention, men. Deception was Satan's goal and he knew Eve would be easier to deceive. That's why he shrewdly chose her instead of Adam. Men, this is why it's so important that our wives have strong, authentic, courageous, and godly husbands. Men they can trust and find safety in. Adam was that man for Eve but now she sees a better way for herself.

As I said earlier, I don't believe Adam was part of the encounter between Eve and the serpent at the start, but I do believe he's there now. I believe that what he has walked into is alarming and startling to him. Adam had just spent possibly a year or more with Eve getting to know her. He'd shared everything with her about the garden, the animals, and God. He'd fallen in love with her. So he'd come to know everything about her and her personality. As husbands and wives can grow to do, he can read her expressions. They know each other well. What he walks up on is a very different woman. She looks, speaks, and acts different. She's visibly under the spell and control of another. He does not recognize the wife he's come to know. He also knows where they are in the garden. At this time they are next to THE TREE. I'm sure his heart is racing and his thoughts are conflicting. This isn't good and he knows it. Adam! Say something! Do something! But he doesn't. Why didn't Adam step in and stop it? Hang on, I have the answer and it reveals much about men. I'll tell you, but first let's finish with Eve.

EVE TAKES THE FRUIT

The next thing the Bible says, *"So she took some of the fruit and ate it" [6]*. I want you to consider something. If this were an apple tree, which a lot of paintings portray, how many apples would they have to eat before it became sin? Obviously the answer is one bite. God told Adam not to eat of the tree, period. Notice what Eve does next. In all my years of Bible study I've not seen this before. She takes "some of the fruit." Most Bible translations indicate she took more than one. It's as though she's thinking, "if one apple will give me wisdom then I'll eat many apples." When Eve lost her way, "greed" took over. She probably has an arm full of apples and one in the other hand being devoured. Again, I believe Adam is in shock. He's watching all this happen and he's silent. Why did Adam remain silent? Here's why, men. Pay close attention. Adam is making the mistaken choice that men are prone to make primarily when it comes to women or their wives. I sure did, and I don't think I'm alone. Adam was silent because of a moment of destructive passive indecision. He knew his wife was in trouble and he knew she was acting out against his and God's stated will and command for them both. But he, like Eve, in a moment, chose to listen to his feelings and ignore God. Men, passivity is our easiest pit to fall into especially when it comes to the woman we love. Stop and think for a minute men, how many regrettable decisions have we made in that moment of passive indecision? There have been many. This is why we must live a "God first life" always.

A man's love for his wife is a strong intoxicating reality. Men will concede, give in, and say yes to a woman when sometimes **no, stop,** is the better way. John and Stasi Eldredge write this in their book *Captivating. "In fact, passivity might make a man safe, but it has done untold damage to women in the long run. It certainly did to Eve. For Adam, his essence is strength in action. That is what he speaks to the world. He bears the image of God, who is a warrior. On behalf of God, Adam says, God will come through. God is on the move. That is why a passive man is so disturbing. His passivity defies his very essence. It violates the way he bears God's image. A passive man says, God will not come through. He is not acting on your behalf."*

I believe this is the dilemma Adam suddenly found himself in. Men, I want you to hear what I'm about to say. In those few moments prior to Eve eating the apple, Adam passively put his wife before his God and all God had told him. In that moment he put Eve and himself first when first place belonged to God. The Bible says in, Exodus 20:3 [3] *"You must not have any other god but me."* This means never ever! I know men, when it comes to the love we have for our wives and family, it is hard not to do this sometimes. But as men we must keep God always first in our lives which means saying no at times to the people we love the most. Think about it, men. If Adam had said NO to Eve and rescued her from Satan the world would be a very different place today.

THE TRUTH OF WHAT I DID
I'm a man so I've failed at this, and as a result I have

two failed marriages. In my first marriage, like Eve, I put me first. And the kicker is, I was a pastor. I should've known better. Like Adam and Eve, I knew what God required. But, I was more concerned with what I wanted. I was so determined to have life my way that I was an angry, controlling, verbally and emotionally abusive man to my family. I thought if I could instill fear in them then I could control them. I learned all that behavior from my angry controlling mother who raised me and treated my father that way. But that's no excuse. I'm a Christian adult man responsible for my behavior. I was wrong. I sinned and I have asked God, my first wife, and my sons to forgive me. I have great admiration for the mother of my two sons for enduring that hell for 27 years.

I was single for the next ten years and in those years something inside of me changed. I mellowed. I still hadn't come to terms with the childhood wounds deep within me, but nevertheless I had changed. I suppose after being raised by an angry controlling mother, after being controlling and verbally abusive to my family for 27 years, I wanted calm and peace in my life. It seemed that calm and peace came naturally to me, like it was who I am. The truth is, it did come naturally because of what I learned from being raised by a passive father who loved and would do anything for my mother even to the point of destruction.

At the end of those ten years I met my second wife. I was pastoring again after being away from it for twelve years. We met in 2013 and we fell in "love" quickly. I tell you, men; I was the total opposite of who I was in my first marriage. It surprised even me. I was notice-ably different to my adult sons. Instead of being the fear instilling, verbally abusive, and controlling husband I was in my first marriage, I was a passive, always compliant, surrendering, and saying yes to everything, husband. For the next seven years I chose passive surrender and giving-in in hopes of pleasing and appeasing her. As in my first marriage I did not lead the way God intended me to do. My wife needed what all wives need. She needed a strong, caring, loving, leader in her life. One who was willing to say no and be firm when needed, but I did what Adam did and put her before God's will for me too many times. After seven years of constant conflict and 18 councilors, we decided enough was enough. To say I learned a lot about me through this is an understatement.

BACK TO THE GARDEN

Now, back to the scene in the garden. The Bible says, *"Then she gave some to her husband, who was with her, and he ate it, too."* Adam still has a choice to make. He could still say no and refuse to eat the fruit. Think about it, what if he had snapped-to and said NO? He would not be a commandment breaker but his wife would. Imagine for a minute what that would be like? But he didn't. In a moment of time he passively complied and became like his wife, a commandment breaker, a sinner.

BEFORE WE GO TO THE NEXT CHAPTER

I want to emphasize a few things about Adam and Eve, husbands and wives, men and women. As I've studied this story, God has clearly shown me my failures as a man. Like Adam, I am incredibly prone to passive behavior. Men, I want you to see that this is every man's tendency. My father was looked at by family and friends as the kindest, gentlest, most considerate man to be known, because he was. To everyone he was that way. He was admired by men, and women wished their husbands were like him. But when it came to my mother he was destructively passive. He's a man. It was his tendency. Because I'm a man, it's my tendency as well and more so because I'm my father's son. I now see it's my biggest struggle. I'm glad I now see it. I say again, men, it was Adam's weakness therefore it's yours. Draw close to God, stay close to God, be the strong authentic man you were created to be. Say NO when needed and show a better way to your wife and family. That's leadership. We must fight for and protect our wives and families from being deceived.

Not only do I firmly believe this story reveals every man's weaknesses, it also reveals every woman's weaknesses and tendencies as well. As it says in a few places in the Bible, Old and New Testaments, it was Eve who was deceived, not Adam. It will be her own confession in the pages to come. Satan used an authoritative approach on Eve because Eve was created to be led by, not only love and care, but strength and authority. God made her that way. Eve listened to another's strong voice and formed a different belief, her new layer. And to her it sounded better. She thought of herself and put her new desires before her husband's and God's.

I experienced this with my mother. She constantly thought of herself first and put her wants and desires before others just as Eve did. These are tendencies and weaknesses of all women. I almost want to "step lightly" when saying this. It's my passivity saying "be nice." But, if it was Eve's tendency, it is every woman's struggle. God will say this directly to her later. God made Eve to be "one flesh" with her husband, to be his other sawhorse. Ladies, draw close to God, stay close to God and you will be able to submit to and follow your husband. If God is not first in your life you will not be able to surrender to your husband.

Men, this is biblical truth. I know it's not what our culture says but we were created to shape our culture, and our culture needs reshaping. In the next chapter we're going to continue this journey through the story of Adam and Eve's fall and learn more about ourselves.

CHAPTER 7

THE MARRIAGE TEMPLATE HAD BEEN FORGED

They've sinned! Paradise is lost, forever. God's design for the garden, all living creatures, and a sinless Adam and Eve is gone. Even though they sinned, God's designed plan for a man and a woman has not been lost. Even though they sinned and paradise in the garden is over, the man, woman, and marriage template has been forged. And we will learn even more about it in the way God justly deals with their sin in the rest of Genesis 3.

In the last chapter I left you with this thought, "what if Adam chose not to eat the fruit?" Now, this next part is my own commentary. It didn't happen this way but just for consideration and based on all our life experiences with relationships, let's consider this for a few minutes. What if Adam comes to his senses and screams NO, STOP and cry's out to God for help? He takes his wife away from the tree where she just ate the fruit, wraps her up in his arms and takes her away to comfort her. This could've happened because the companion of every follower of God which Adam was, is God the Holy Spirit. The Bible says one of the Holy Spirit's jobs is to convict. He reminds us of what's right and wrong before and right up to committing sin. John 14:26 says, *"But when the Father sends the Advocate as my representative that is, the Holy Spirit he will teach you everything and will remind you of everything I have told you."* And in John 16:8 it says, *"And when he comes, he will convict the world of its sin, and of God's righteousness, and of the coming judgment."* Adam did not have the Holy Spirit living in him as we do because of our salvation, but God himself was with him in the garden and Adam knew the truth. So, at the very moment before Adam ate the fruit I believe he was being convicted and reminded of all that God had told him. To say that Adam was in an avalanche of internal conflict is a huge understatement. He's watching his beloved be assaulted with manipulation. She's just done what God told him they must not do. He's frozen with love for her and a desire to please God, but she's right there. He's standing next to her when she hands him the fruit. In a split moment of time he gives in, eats the fruit and joins her in sin. It's what love stories and paperback novels are made of. BUT WAIT! STOP! This is real life with real life consequences. As Christians and Bible people we've all heard the term "we live in a fallen world." The garden, as recorded in Genesis 3, is when our current fallen world fell.

. . .

GOD STEPS IN

Now, let's look at what God teaches every man and woman, husband and wife, today through Adam and Eve's redemption process. God does not throw up His hands and say, "That does it! We have to start all over." Because of His love for them He continues with them just like He'll do with us.

Adam and Eve chose to sin on their own. They experienced the effects of sin, then God steps in. It is important that every follower of Christ understand God's redemption process. To understand it through Adam and Eve's story we must look closely at their sin, the effects of their sin, their response to God, and what God does for them and with them.

Their sin was doing what God said not to do, disobeying Him, and eating the fruit. Too often we want to call what Eve did, listening to and being drawn in by Satan, sin. Too often we want to call her a sinner because she failed to leave and run to her husband. Too often we want to lay the blame of sin on Adam because he chose not to step in and rescue Eve. We want to say Adam sinned as he was in a struggle with his love for Eve and for God. But the Bible says sin occurred when the fruit was eaten. All that drama between Eve and the serpent, and between Adam and Eve was the temptation process. Remember, being tempted is not sin. It's the giving in to temptation that's sin. As a preacher, I've made this mistake, calling what Eve and Adam did before eating the fruit sin. But God said in Genesis 2:17, *"If you eat its fruit, you are sure to die."* It is certainly not good to allow ourselves to be tempted. We should run from it! They didn't and sin was the result.

THE DEADLY EFFECTS OF THEIR SIN

The deadly effects of their sin is death. Genesis 3:6-7 says, [6] *"... So she took some of the fruit and ate it. Then she gave some to her husband, who was with her, and he ate it, too. [7] At that moment their eyes were opened, and they suddenly felt shame at their nakedness..."* When was the moment that "their eyes were opened?" Men, you must see this. We as men must fully understand the weight of the responsibility God has placed on all men. This weighty responsibility hasn't changed over these thousands of years. Although culture and views have changed in regards to men and women, what God originally established has not. It wasn't until Adam ate the fruit that the Bible then says *"their eyes were opened and they felt shame."* As I've said earlier, if Adam had suddenly snapped-to and not eaten the fruit it would've been only Eve guilty of sin. Adam, the first image bearer would still be in good standing with God. But, that's not the way it happened. The knowledge and the effects of sin hit them hard and sudden. In an instant their eyes and awarenesses were open. They suddenly know and feel things they weren't made to know. They know by sudden experience shame, guilt, and fear. This is the "death" that God warned Adam of when He said, *"If you eat its fruit, you are sure to die"* [2:17]. Their life with God and each other in the garden ended, died. Sin brings death! The first part of Romans 6:23 says, *"For the wages of sin is death, but the free gift of God is eternal life through Christ Jesus our Lord."* And the moment of death came when Adam, not Eve, ate the fruit.

It's important that all men see this. It was Adam that God directly told not to eat the fruit of this tree. It was Adam that heard the words of God and it was Adam that shared these same words with Eve. God had placed Adam in charge of the garden, every tree in it, all the animals, his wife, and all the responsibility that came with it. So, the moment that Adam ate the fruit, the effects of sin gripped them both. Yes, Eve by her choices put him in that spot. Adam didn't create this storm, Satan and Eve did. This was her doing. But Adam had the same power of choice Eve had, and he failed. Brothers, as men with God's help, He places us in charge of our life, our wives, our children, our homes, and our vocations. And with that charge comes a holy responsibility. All men today and forever have this same responsibility. It's God given! Men, we need to be living as the God Made Man we are. Our families and current culture desperately needs strong godly men. We see this clearly through Adam and Eve's story.

A COMMON RESPONSE TO SIN

Their response to their sin is common to all of us. Verse 7 says, *"So they sewed fig leaves together to cover themselves."* Men, notice something here, no one is leading. Adam, who was appointed by God to lead his family has lost his bearings, he's lost his way. "Sin's job" is to render you aimless. Adam and Eve are scrambling aimlessly to fix what they've done. What do they do? They take matters into their own hands. Prior to this sin event they had a wonderful, growing, and fulfilling relationship with God and each other. They spent time together. They walked and talked together. Now, they're thrust into a situation they've never experienced, and feelings they've never felt. So now they do what's common to all of us. They don't go to God with their failures because of fear. They turn to themselves and run away from God in guilt and shame. Together they sinned so together they do the same thing to cover their shame and nakedness. Prior to their sin, Adam was the confident courageous loving leader of their lives. Now, they are in chaos together. God's order is lost. Let's face it, because we now live in a "fallen world" there will be challenges and struggles in our lives. There will always be a need for strong godly men to lead. Therefore we must be men in constant pursuit of God. Men, I said earlier, Satan will be part of your world the rest of your life. Not only must we lead in the way we follow God, we must also lead by example in the way we seek Him when we fail.

Thank God that He is God! He is the ultimate strong but compassionate example for all of us to follow. Men, we find in the way God addressed these sinners, their sin, and their redemption the way we are to lead our lives and families. Remember, we men and women are God's image bearers. Not only do we bear His image by obeying him, we bear His image by imitating him. The way God handles the first sinners shows us how we should react to those who sin against us. Have you ever looked at this story this way? I sure haven't, but I see it now.

GOD WALKS TOWARD THEM

Genesis 3:8 says, *"When the cool evening breezes were blowing, the man and his wife heard the LORD God walking about in the garden. So they hid from the LORD God among the trees."* Notice what God doesn't do. He could've stomped around throwing down lighting, thunder, hale, fire, and brimstone. From Adam and Eve's response it seems they were expecting God's wrath. Let's face it, when we're wronged those are the emotions many of us feel. We want to retaliate against our offender. Too many times husbands and wives approach each other and their families this way. But not God. Let's consider why He approached them the way He did. God knew they were in an emotional state they had never been in. They are experiencing guilt, shame, and fear for the first time. They are in hiding, hiding from the lover of their lives. So God walks gently toward them. The Bible says *"when the cool evening breezes were blowing."* It's as though you could almost hear the sounds of a lullaby playing in the back ground, not the attack music from Jaws. Imagine how much more terrified and fearful they would've been if God approached them in right-eous anger stomping through the garden. This is why God The Father, the Son, and the Holy Spirit is every man's example. Let's be honest here, men, too many of us approach others and our families with demonstra-tions of anger and all our anger does is make things worse and damage the people we love. I remember a couple of years ago coming home from church, rounding a corner and coming upon an accident. A seventeen year old boy had lost control of his mother's SUV and wrecked into a fence. He was stunned but okay, though very nervous. As I tried to comfort him he said he was worried about what his dad was going to do. I tried to assure him it would be okay. Minutes later his father drives up. The boy was the only one prepared for what happened next because he knew his father. To my horror his father lunges at his son screaming and cursing at him for wrecking his mother's car. The young man stood there like a scared puppy saying "yes sir." The father never once asked if he was hurt or okay. The young man was visibly shaken from his father's abuse and had to ride home with a friend after his father left him and drove away. Brothers, I'm so glad that the God who loves us never treats us this way. I'm guilty of out of control anger in my first marriage, and I destroyed it. Brothers, you alone can change the culture of your family and home by the way you approach them. Although this book is written to men, women and mothers must learn God's approach to husbands and families as well. Let God be our example.

HE CALLED OUT TO THEM

Genesis 3:9 says, *"Then the LORD God called to the man, "Where are you?"* This is SO important for every man to see. The garden is in crisis, paradise has fallen, and God's ultimate creation, man and woman, are hiding from God in fear for their lives. Who does God call out to? Adam! Why doesn't He call out to Eve, she sinned first? Why didn't He call out to both of them, they both sinned? Here's why. Because Adam had a one on one relationship with God, and he was responsible. This responsibility wasn't something Adam had earned or achieved. God placed it on him because he's the man, God's first image bearer. God chose it to be this way and He hasn't changed. Men, like Adam, you are responsible for your life and your family. You are answerable to God for them. It's time every man starts listening to God and answering to Him again. This will change your life and culture.

HE QUESTIONS THEM

Let's take a look at the reasons for these questions. Genesis 3:9-13 says, [9] *"Then the LORD God called to the man, "Where are you?" [10] He replied, "I heard you walking in the garden, so I hid. I was afraid because I was naked." [11] "Who told you that you were naked?" the LORD God asked. "Have you eaten from the tree whose fruit I commanded you not to eat?" [12] The man replied, "It was the woman you gave me who gave me the fruit, and I ate it." [13] Then the LORD God asked the woman, "What have you done?" "The serpent deceived me," she replied. That's why I ate it."*

The first question was appropriately asked to Adam, *"where are you?"* Let's consider some things here. God wasn't asking this because He couldn't find Adam. He was not waiting for Adam to raise his trembling hand

and say "I'm over here." God knew his location in the garden. I believe this was a "self-examination" prompting question. "Adam do you know where you are in relationship with me? Do you know what you have done? Do you feel the "death pain" of our separa-tion? Do you feel My disappointment?" I believe this is the basic fundamental question God holds for and directs to every man who fails in his GOD GIVEN responsibilities. And brothers, because of Adam's failure we will fail. I don't say this to give us an excuse. I say this to remind us that God is our creator and He holds us to His original plan, and when we fail we must go to God, not run from Him.

The second question was asked Adam. Adam had said, *"I was afraid because I was naked."* [11] *"Who told you that you were naked?" the LORD God asked."* God asks, "who told you…?" In other words, "who have you been listening to?" For one, he was not listening to the familiar voice of God and two, he listened to his wife and took and ate the fruit. Then the influence of the liar came flooding in. It was Adam's sin that caused the death of separation from God. He's now completely exposed to the shrewd lying voice of Satan. Men, it can't be stressed enough to know the word of God in your life, listen to His words, and obey them. As with Adam, this is our endless responsibility. But when we sin and fail our responsibility, then what? Listen closely, this next part is what God will do for all of us and we must respond as Adam did.

. . .

GOD CONFRONTS THEIR SIN

God the Spirit engages with us through conviction before we sin, and He will confront our sin afterwards. After God has led Adam to experience his failure He then goes straight to the core issue, *"Have you eaten from the tree whose fruit I commanded you not to eat?"* It needs to be pointed out that God didn't ask Adam why he didn't step in to stop and rescue Eve. Yes he should've but Eve's sin was NOT the result of Adam's passivity. Her sin was her own choice. Again, God's question wasn't asked because He didn't know the answer. It was asked to give Adam a choice, "are you going to own it or not?" This is what God The Holy Spirit does for all who sin. When we find ourselves in that emotionally unsettled place after we sin, or when we finally realize our failure after years of denial, that's God giving you a chance to own it because, my friend, your sin is yours alone. Men, we must quit dragging the weight of sin and failure through our lives. Come clean before God and if necessary come clean to the people you need to forgive or seek forgiveness from.

I did this with my first wife many years after our divorce. I sought God's forgiveness and He forgave me. Then, I decided to take a four day getaway to pray and do "business" with God. I hooked up to my RV and went to a Texas state park for the purpose of writing five letters of confession and seeking forgiveness. One each to my deceased father and mother, one to each of my two adult sons, and one to my first wife. The first day was spent praying that God would show me what to say. After four days the only letter I could write was to the mother of my two sons. I poured my heart out to her OWNING my failure. I ended it with seeking her forgiveness. Whether or not she forgave me doesn't matter. I did what I needed to do as a man. I should've done this many years ago. Brothers, it's never too late to do the right thing.

When God asked Adam *"have you eaten from the tree..."* He was doing what God the Spirit does when we sin. He goes straight to the issue. He didn't ask, "Adam what have you done?" He puts His divine finger on it. Like with all of us He wants Adam to see it. Adam had a choice, own it, deny it, or blame Eve. This is what God does for us men and a God Made Man owns his failures and does the right thing.

ADAM AND EVE GIVE AN ANSWER

In Genesis 3:12 Adam says, *"It was the woman you gave me who gave me the fruit, and I ate it."* Now, there's two ways to look at this. One, you can say that Adam gives in to the temptation to pass the buck and place part of the blame on Eve. Let's face it, we've all been tempted to pass the blame. I've heard Bible teachers say that this is what Adam is doing. I disagree, and here's why. I believe Adam accepts full responsibility for his own actions. He said, *"and I ate it."* Adam knows who God is. God's the one who formed him and breathed HIS life into him. The two of them had a rich friendship and relationship. Therefore, Adam is not passing the buck and he's not blaming God for giving her to him. God asks a straight forward question and Adam gives a factual answer. "Here's how it happened God, the woman you gave me gave me the fruit and I ate it." I don't believe Adam is blaming Eve, and he's certainly not blaming God. I believe he's remembering God told HIM not to eat the fruit and he's confessing how it happened and what he did. Neither Adam nor any of us will ever "get one past God." Adam was not passing the buck because he was not deceived by Eve. He failed as a husband, he sinned and he owned his sin. That's why God says what He says next.

GOD QUESTIONS EVE

He then turns to Eve and asks, *"what have you done?"* [3:13] In other words, "Eve, do you see what you have done?" Notice that God doesn't ask Eve the same question He asked Adam. He asked Adam *"have you eaten from the tree I told you not to eat."* It was Adam God gave this command to, and it was Adam that had the responsibility of telling Eve, which he did. I say again it was Eve who was deceived not Adam. Look carefully at her answer to God. *"The serpent deceived me, that's why I ate it."* Adam didn't say his wife deceived him. That would've been shifting the blame to her. However, Eve does blame the serpent for deceiving her. Then she admits that's why she ate the fruit. Eve does not take responsibility for her choice. She doesn't own it as her own sin. That's why it says later in the New Testament, 1 Timothy 2:13-14 [13] *"For God made Adam first, and afterward he made Eve. [14] And it was not Adam who was deceived by Satan. The woman was deceived, and sin was the result."* Eve was given the same opportunity to confess and own her sin as Adam was given. This was her sin and hers alone but she blames the deceiver, she blames someone else for her failure and refuses to own it. And, there is no biblical record that she ever owned her sin. This gives us a look into the heart and mind of Eve. She was given the same opportunity to confess and own her sin but she refuses to. Why did she refuse to own her sin? Why did she stick with her first response to God? Was it stubbornness? I don't know, but it reveals something unsettling about Eve.

THE CORE PROBLEM IN OUR CULTURE

Ladies and gentlemen, even though this happened in the beginning it remains the core problem in our culture today. Shifting blame for our own choices is a common temptation for all of us. It is human nature to cover up, not to accept responsibility, and blame others. But according to the Old and New Testament it first happened with Eve. This is why our culture needs strong, authentic, God-following men. Men who follow God first and take full responsibility for their life, their families, and their failures. Adam sinned and he confessed it and owned it as his alone.

The world we live in will remain a fallen broken world until it's over and we're with Jesus. But until then the culture of our lives, the culture of our families, and the cultures we live in can be changed and must be changed by authentic God-Made-Men doing the right thing. Men, I implore you. Humble yourselves before

God. Bring your sins to him and do the right thing. Step up, man up, and step into your God given responsibilities and lead as God wants to lead you according to His word.

Men, I'm so glad Adam owned his sin. It was imperative that he did. He was the one, the only one, that God told about the tree of *"knowledge and of good and evil."* Adam was the one that heard God say *"you must not eat it."* So the man Adam did the right thing, he confessed his sin to God. Adam's confession opened the door to what we will see in the next chapter.

Some of you are are still struggling with unconfessed sin. It may be something you're involved in now. It may be something in your past that you've kept hidden. It is never too late for a man to do the right thing. Listen to the voice of God. Bring your failures to Him. He will forgive you! Listen more, and do what He tells you to do.

CHAPTER 8

GOD'S ORDER IS RESTORED

God is just and He is sovereign. He is good and He is loving, so loving that He does not give up on His plan for His first image bearers. For Adam and Eve there must be a reckoning. There must be forgiveness and redemption. The sin of Adam and Eve must be fully dealt with. This is what we see in the rest of Genesis 3. Men, pay close attention to what God says to Eve and to Adam. Pay attention to what God says about Eve. When or if you ever hear the term "Eve's curse," you must forever understand it wasn't just on her. Eve's curse is on every woman. Even the one you're married to or will be married to. This is what the Bible says. Pay close attention to what God says about Adam. God firmly states again Adam's relationship role with Eve. This wasn't only for them, it is for every married man and woman today. And, pay close attention to what God says about Adam's curse. He was banished from the garden, the good life that God designed for him. God places the burden and responsibility on the man to work hard to provide and care for his wife and family. Men, Satan wants to destroy you and keep you from fulfilling God's purpose for your life, but as you'll see, God's plan for you and your Eve is redeemed.

THE IMPORTANCE OF ORDER AND PRIORITY

I've said often that priority and order is important to God. In Genesis 3:14 and following, God starts the reckoning and He begins where the fall began, with the serpent. The Bible says, *"Then the LORD God said to the serpent, Because you have done this, you are cursed more than all animals, domestic and wild."* God knows who the deceiver is. He didn't, all of a sudden, discover it during His questioning of Adam and Eve. God knew all along. With Adam and Eve, God asks questions to help them see what they have done. Not with the serpent. He starts with him and justly punishes what he did. He started where the offense began.

God then addresses Eve, the first sinner. Remember, Eve did not "own" her sin. She blamed the serpent. Genesis 3:16 says, *"Then he said to the woman, 'I will sharpen the pain of your pregnancy, and in pain you will give birth. And you will desire to control your husband, but he will rule over you"* (NLT). Eve was already able to bare children. Child birth was already going to be uncomfortably difficult. So God sharpens her pain of pregnancy and childbirth. All mothers understand this. But then God says something that too many have never fully understood or have simply chosen to ignore. As I've researched this, it's been interesting to read and listen to how men delicately and softly address the second part of verse 16. They try to be careful and not offensive. So let me say this, it's not my intention to be deliberately offensive but I am most definitely trying to be biblically accurate and thorough. Let's be honest, God's words are strong, direct, and are offensive to anyone who offends. The biblical truths found in the second part of verse 16 explain so much about marriages and the husband and wife relationship today. God speaks bluntly, clearly, and directly to both. He uses few words, but they speak volumes. And ladies and gentlemen, the sooner we get and understand this the sooner we'll be on our way to finding God's balance and health for marriage.

The second part of Eve's curse is this, *"And you will desire to control your husband but he will rule over you."* The ESV says, *"Your desire shall be contrary to your husband, but he shall rule over you."* These are not the words of a man, a husband, or some Bible teacher. These are the words of God Himself.

I grew up in church literally all my life. Denominational and nondenominational churches both, and I can honestly say teaching on this topic was not covered. As a pastor of twenty seven years I never addressed it. Ignoring biblical truth is the reason that even in the church there is marital strife, and it should not be because we have the truth. We must do as Jesus taught, go back to the beginning and do what God originally said. God gives the reason marriages will have problems and He gives the answer. As we look deeper into this listen for the answer.

I believe a spotlight needs to be shown on this statement in verse 16. Notice God says *"you will desire to control your husband or, your desire will be contrary to your husband."* God said this exclusively to and about Eve. In other words, this will be an ongoing struggle with Adam and Eve and within every woman therefore every marriage. We've just seen it happen as Eve chose to do contrarily to what her husband told her. She stepped from under Adam's protective authority and decided to handle "the situation" herself by eating the fruit, which resulted in sin. This is going to be her ongoing struggle that they both will have to deal with. The fourth chapter of Genesis will give you insight as to the disfunction in Adam's family. And it will be an ongoing issue in every marriage forward. Ladies and gentlemen, I think sometimes we act as though this was only Adam and Eve's struggle because of their sin. But no, just like the rainbow will always show in rainy skies, childbearing will always be very sharp and painful, and every man's responsibility will be to work and provide; the struggle for control, the struggle for who will lead the home, the temptation to discount the husband's role, the desire to do contrarily or opposite the husband will be a constant marital struggle. From Eve and forward, it will be every woman's curse therefore every marriage's struggle. No woman can dare say, "this is not me, this is not who I am." God and the Bible says it is, and every man must understand this. Men, the majority of women will reject this. I believe God said this to Eve in the presence of Adam. He knew this about Eve because of personal experience, and he heard God say it. This is why my encouragement to all men is to understand and know this real truth. The more truth you know will help you understand your role as a husband.

John F. MacArthur says this about Genesis 3:16 in his MacArthur Bible Commentary. "Sin has turned the harmonious system of God-ordained roles into distasteful struggles of self-will. Lifelong companions, husbands and wives, will need God's help in getting along as a result. The woman's desire will be to lord it over her husband, but the husband will rule by divine design."

One of my favorite people to read is John Piper. He says this about Genesis 3:16, "So what is really described in the curse of Genesis 3:16 is the ugly conflict between the male and female that has marked so much of human history. Maleness as God created it has been depraved and corrupted by sin. Femaleness as God created it has been depraved and corrupted by sin. The essence of sin is self-reliance and self-exaltation. First in rebellion against God, and then in exploitation of each other."

As I said earlier, I've made the same mistakes that we see in Adam and Eve's story. I've experienced those struggles of self-will in my two marriages. I've experienced the struggle and results of control and passivity. But we, husbands and wives, were made by God to live according to His will and purposes. Even in the culture we live in, we can, we must, be the men and women God originally made us to be.

ALL IS NOT LOST

There is great hope for the marriage relationship today. We can experience God's plan and live together as He designed. Two reasons. First, these next words are written to all post resurrection Christians. We have the ever-indwelling presence of the Holy Spirit in us. The one who empowers and helps us is in us. We just have to listen to Him. Second, in Genesis 3:16 God resets the order. Even though they both sinned, their sin did not erase God's created order, purpose, and plan. Remember I said earlier, "Listen for the answer," here it is. God said, "But he (Adam, husband) shall rule over you." I say again, God said this to Eve in the presence of Adam. I know, that word "rule" is a deal breaker for today's culture. The idea of husbands "ruling" their wives is a scary notion to women today. It conjures up images of dictators and tyrants. But we have to face the fact that the word "rule" was used by God, so let's understand it. I don't want men to read Genesis 3:16 and get the wrong idea, and I don't want women to fear it. God used a strong word, "rule," as He reset the order of things. The word "rule" means to <u>have dominion, responsibility, and reign over</u>. It describes what God told Adam to do with the garden and the animals. God brought each animal to Adam and later He brings Eve to Adam. This is strong language, but strength is what's needed in light of what happened with Adam and Eve.

It was never God's intention for a man to rule his wife as a dictator or tyrant. Remember, God is our example and we've just seen how He rules as He deals lovingly and strongly with Adam and Eve's sin. God was purposeful, He was direct, and authoritative in ruling Adam and Eve, and He was loving. God is putting things back in their proper order. In 1 Corinthians 11:3 Paul says, *"But I want you to understand that the head of every man is Christ, the head of a wife is her husband, and the head of Christ is God."* The one who "rules" has a heavy responsibility to lead as God leads him. And God was making it clear to Eve therefore to every woman that His order was still in place.

These are the last words He says to Eve before He addresses Adam's sin. It's as though God gathered all the scattered building blocks caused by their sin, picked up block number one and said to Eve, "I have given you to your husband. I have given your husband, authority and responsibility over you. He answers to only Me on behalf of you. This is the order I've created for you both to live under." Men, this has not changed. As a man you have leadership responsibility and authority over your wife, home, and vocation. You didn't design it, God did. You didn't ask for it, God assigned it to you. Therefore it will work and work well if we <u>both</u> obey God's word. So no matter your failures, men, it is on you to step in, man up, and lead your wife and family with confidence and courage as God made you to lead.

I found these words from John Piper's "Desiring God" website written by Jason DeRouchie. "According to the paradigm that Genesis 1–3 sets forth, the wife is the helper who is not domineering, manipulative, coercive, passive, or destructive. Instead, she is characterized by honoring and respecting her husband with a heart of service and by a genuine contribution to the two-person team that complements the husband's strengths and weaknesses. Similarly, God calls the husband to lead his home, serving as the primary provider and protector both physically and spiritually. He should lead by convictional, sacrificial love, not in a way that is domineering, manipulative, coercive, passive, or destructive. In Ephesians 5:22–33, Paul identifies that the distinct callings that husbands and wives have in marriage display the distinct callings within the relationship of Christ and His church. Christ's glory is at stake in how husbands and wives relate!"

NOW ADAM HEARS FROM GOD

The last person God deals with is Adam. The serpent was the first deceiver. Eve was the one deceived and the first sinner. Adam was the second to sin and the third to hear from God directly, in this instance. God says to Adam, Genesis 3, [17] *And to the man he said, "Since you listened to your wife and ate from the tree whose fruit I commanded you not to eat, the ground is cursed because of you. All your life you will struggle to scratch a living from it. [18] It will grow thorns and thistles for you, though you will eat of its grains. [19] By the sweat of your brow will you have food to eat until you return to the ground from which you were made. For you were made from dust, and to dust you will return."*

Notice the first thing God says to Adam—*"Since you listened to your wife."* Remember that moment when Adam was standing next to Eve. She may have uttered her thoughts out loud, "Adam, see how delicious the fruit looks. We can be like God and have His wisdom, and I want it." The Bible doesn't say she said these words out loud to Adam but we do know she thought them because the Bible says *"The woman was convinced. She saw that the tree was beautiful and its fruit looked delicious, and she wanted the wisdom it would give her"* [Genesis 3:6]. Look how deceived she was. She believed there was wisdom in the fruit. We do know she said something to Adam because God says to him, *"Since you listened to your wife."* Men, God is not saying we should never listen to our wives. Our wives are created for us, to help us. We need their companionship and assistance in life. A man is a blessed man if he has a smart intelligent wife. But what God tells a man to do, as He did Adam, is that he must not let his wife nor anyone else convince him otherwise. Being in the place of leadership and authority that God puts you in requires doing only what God tells you to do.

Adam now has to work, labor, and struggle to provide for himself and family. Before the fall, life was really good. God provided everything they needed. They lived in the garden, ate from the garden, and walked with God in harmony everyday. Once the fall happened, that was lost. The living we make today, men, must be earned. This wasn't the case before the fall.

ADAM STEPS BACK INTO HIS PLACE OF LEADERSHIP

Genesis 3:20 says, *"Then the man Adam named his wife Eve, because she would be the mother of all who live."* In Genesis 2 Adam calls her "woman" because she came from him. Adam now steps back into his God given place of leadership responsibility and gives his wife her name, "Eve." He recognizes her identity and purpose in life. Aside from helping him she will bear his children.

THEY ARE NOW READY FOR WHAT GOD DOES NEXT

So now God has dealt with their sin. They know their punishment. Adam takes back his responsibility and leads his wife. He honors her with giving her her name. They now stand ready for what God does next. God forgives them. Please hear this, men. Forgiveness and restoration is ours when we confess and repent. Forgiveness was given them because Adam owned his sin [Genesis 3:12]. If he hadn't, there would not be forgiveness for either of them. Verse 21 says, *"And the LORD God made clothing from animal skins for Adam and his wife."* God took perfect innocent animals, He shed their blood for Adam and Eve and HE clothed them with their skins. Their own attempt to clothe themselves came from guilt and fear. God clothed them with love and forgiveness. I love this! In this we see tenderness, compassion, and completeness. This is how God deals with the repentant heart. Men, God the Father, God the Son, and God the Holy Spirit is our example. We must put Him first in our lives and follow Him.

I, like Adam, have sinned. I've made a mess of too many things in my life. I have disappointed others, my family, and most importantly, God. But the shed blood of Jesus Christ has forgiven me. As I look into my future now I'm encouraged! I like the path God has me on. I have never been as confident as I am now about the last part of my life and it's all because of what God has been showing and teaching me about myself and authentic manhood. I want to live as the man He made me to be! I want the same for YOU. Our lives and marriages depend on each of us being the God Made Man He made us to be.

In the next chapters I want to share my journey with you that started at the beginning of 2021. I'm going to share my personal journaling as God spoke to me week by week. In the following chapter I'll share what I believe was the biggest dilemma in my life at the time, my bitterness. The bitterness and unforgiveness I held against my wife had to be faced. No matter what happened with my marriage, the bitterness that was consuming me needed to end. When our separation began this was my primary focus.

In chapter 10 I'll share more of my journaling and what I believe are my greatest lessons learned about myself. These lessons have literally liberated me. I finally received answers to decades-long questions about myself. My prayer is that all who read this will learn what I've learned.

I'm just one man, nobody special except to God and my family. But as a man my eyes have been opened. I have the rest of my life to be a real man, the man God made me to be. I hope and pray that the words of this book and the story of my journey have encouraged you to seek God and embrace The-God-Made-Man you are.

CHAPTER 9

BITTERNESS IS A PRISON
My Healing Journey From Bitterness
(from my personal journal.)

What you are going to read is my journaling as God walked me through my anger and bitterness. I've kept it exactly as I experienced it with the exception of name deletions.

A little back story is required first. For the past seven years I was pastoring the church that my wife and I started. Relational conflict began between us before we married. Sadly, the church became one of our major points of conflict. When I say conflict, I'm not talking about marital spats and arguments. These were not physical but were extremely verbally and emotionally explosive. I have never been spoken to nor heard such hurtful expressions used against me in my life as I experienced with her. Not even from my abusive mother. My wife would explode, I would go quiet and passive. Eventually I'd stand up for myself; push repeat every two weeks for seven plus years. Soon these problems began to spill over into the church. After seven years of this it came to a head when my wife said she was divorcing me and wanted to share it with the church. I said no, but that we will meet with the elders. On the first Sunday of January 2021, the meeting was held after church. My friend Trampus oversaw the meeting. She announced to the elders she was divorcing me and at the end of the meeting I resigned the church. One of the good men who was an elder stepped in to pastor and I'm happy to say the church is doing well.

Our second separation started after that first Sunday in January, 2021. I moved out of the house and into our RV toward the back of the property. All I wanted to do is be alone with God. My heart was hurting. I needed answers. So I poured myself into prayer and God's word. I was on a mission. I was full of resentment and bitterness toward my wife after seven painful years of relational conflict. It was the most painful seven years of my life. I knew I was drowning in bitterness toward my wife and I wanted to be free from that. So I began. For the next month, I sought God for His help. I knew what I was feeling was eating me up from the inside. Whether or not our marriage would be saved was no longer the issue. The issue was me; the issue was in me. What I was feeling in my heart toward my wife was wrong and I knew it. My anger, resentment, and bitterness was my number one problem. Not only was it distorting the way I related to and saw my wife, I realized it was interfering with my relationship with God. Finding help from Him became my singular focus. Focusing on saving my marriage was not my primary concern at this time. Me and God and my healing and wholeness had to be my focus, and I knew it.

The following is the journaling I did through this. Every waking hour was devoted to this. I've left in the websites I searched and read. As I write this now and look back, I will be forever thankful to God for freeing me from the chokehold of bitterness. Men, if this is your problem I hope and pray you do the same. Get free from bitterness and unforgiveness toward anyone in your life. It will make you a better man. The words you're about to read are as they came to me. It was very personal as though God sat me down and said, "I want to show you what you need to see."

From My Journal

January 4, 2021

I will never be able to see this clearly and cleanly until my *sin* is faced, and dealt with through confession, repentance, and forgiveness. (Thank you for your divine help, Lord. You promise your help to those who confess, repent and trust you)

My path while separated....

God has been calling me to a place of being alone with Him consistently for some time now. He wants to minister to me like the one sheep who has gone astray.

I know that my struggle with my wife is bitterness that I've allowed to grow in me due to my unwillingness to forgive her. I've held on to the hurt she's done to me. I replay the hurts in my head as a justification for the way I feel. I KNOW this, and this is the problem I must seek God about. So, I began. I prayed. I decided to learn about bitterness in a person. I wanted to learn from clinical psychology and Christian psychology together. What I learned from both groups is what the Bible clearly teaches, bitterness is born out of unforgiveness. I KNOW THIS and I know that the bitterness in me toward my wife is due to my not forgiving her of all the hurt she has done to me. I fell into a trap of my own making. I'd say to myself, "she's just going to do it again." I lived in fear and full expectation of it happening again, so forgiving seemed useless. My bitterness grew!

This week has been a good journey with God. He first led me to Psalm 25. That was cool in itself! I was looking for Psalm 29. As I finished reading I realized it was Psalm 25. It was just what I needed and God knew it. It was as though He sat me down in front of Psalm 25. I've made that Psalm my prayer everyday.

I called my wife, I think Wednesday the 6th or Thursday the 7th, and shared what God was showing me. I confessed my bitterness due to unforgiveness, and asked her to forgive me. It was not a long conversation, I just felt I needed to let her know what I was doing and that I was seeking the Lord.

Below are the web articles I found and read, and my corresponding notes.

https://www.psychologytoday.com/us/blog/evolu

tion-the-self/201501/don-t-let-your-anger-mature-bitterness

I know it's wrong (sin) to hold "hurts done to me" against my wife. So, I CHOOSE not to hold them against her any longer and I choose to forgive her. IT IS A CHOICE!! I know that forgiving her is for me to do more than for her. My forgiving her releases us from my prison.

From the articles......

"Virtually every writer who has weighed in on the subject of bitterness has discussed its ultimate remedy: forgiveness. Forgiveness alone enables you to let go of grievances, grudges, rancor, and resentment. As already suggested, the longer you hold onto your anger, the more you'll sink into the destructive quagmire of ever-cycling feelings of hatred and resentment. The more, over time, your anger will mature into bitterness."

https://www.christianitytoday.com/biblestudies/articles/spiritualformation/bitterness-resentment.html

My words.....

When you realize God has forgiven you ALL YOUR SINS and has become your savior at your request, in light of this, forgiving anyone of "wrongs done to you" should be WHO WE ARE AS CHRISTIANS. Matthew 18:24-35 teaches us that the bigger (impossible debt) that was forgiven enables us and should encourage us to forgive all others their sins (debts) against us. My wife's treatment against me is SO much smaller in comparison to my sin against

Jesus. Jesus freely forgave me and continues to show me mercy.

When we have an unforgiving heart, our eyes are not on Jesus; they are fixed on ourselves.

Thought...

"BECAUSE OF THE CROSS, GOD FORGIVES ME SO I FORGIVE YOU. I MUST FORGIVE BECAUSE GOD FORGIVES ME."

My words......

I know my wife does what she does out of deep hurt and wounding in her own life (I pray she finds healing and peace in that). Therefore, I can't hold unforgiveness against her because I too am hurt and wounded from life. Jesus bore my sins, He was wounded, hurt, beaten, murdered/crucified. He took all my sins on himself. He has forgiven me! I think this is how I must see my wife and understand our relationship. When hurt, I need to respond as Jesus would, in compassion toward her. I need to be quick to forgive, I need to resist holding on to hurt, I need to see it as Jesus sees it, sin He has already paid for and forgiven. Jesus does not recoil at my sin.

My sin doesn't set him back on His heels. Jesus leans into me even more. He goes and seeks the lost sheep. He called Zachias to come to him. He called 12 sinners to follow him. He agreed to Nicodemus's condition and met with him privately at night. Jesus moves toward the sinner in their sin, not away from them. This is how I must be to my wife when I feel sinned against by her, love her as Christ loves the church. My natural instincts and learned behavior is to recoil, defend myself, and run, the very opposite of what I should do and what she needs. "Dear God, please help me do the right thing!"

We must be quick to do the "right thing" for each other in the moment conflict presents itself.

https://www.biblicalcounselingcoalition.org/2014/02/21/the-heart-of-bitterness/

BELOW ARE THE WORDS FOUND IN THIS WEB ARTICLE. WOW, THIS BLESSED ME. I COMMIT TO READING IT EVERYDAY.

"Bitterness is focused on what has been done to you. To break up bitterness, you must also be willing to look at what you have done to others. Your task is to admit what your responsibility is in the matter and go to those you have hurt, confess your sin, and first seek their forgiveness. You must be willing to get the log out of your own eye prior to examining your neighbor's eye."

"The examination process begins right here at home. Start with yourself and seek God's help in revealing the contents of your heart in relation to how you have sinned against others."

"Search me, O God, and know my heart; test me and know my thoughts. Point out anything in me that offends you, and lead me along the path of everlasting life." Psalm 139:23-24 (NLT)

(This examination process has been what God has been calling me to for some time now. I've needed this. BR)

There needs to be a willingness on your part to **forsake** your sin of bitterness.

"**Get rid of all** bitterness, rage, anger, harsh words, and slander, as well as all types of malicious behavior.

And be kind to one another, tenderhearted, forgiving one another, even as God in Christ forgave you." Ephesians 4:31-32 (NLT)

Confession of your own sin and repentance for that sin must take place in your heart first. *Then you must seek for other relationships to be healed and restored.* You may want to pray a prayer similar to this one:

"Gracious Heavenly Father, I realize now that I have a root of bitterness in my heart. Thank You that You have chosen this time in my life to reveal it to me. I ask for Your help, dear Lord, to see the areas of my heart and life where bitterness has grown. I trust the Holy Spirit will reveal to me my sin and I confess to you the sin of bitterness regarding the following circumstances in my life : my relationship with my wife, the hurts caused by fights and quarrels, things she has said to me. It has turned to bitterness, I know forgiveness is my answer. SO I FORGIVE HER AND CHOOSE NOT TO ALLOW BITTERNESS TO COME IN.

Thank You, dear Lord, for revealing to me the areas of my life over which I am bitter. Please help me to overcome this sin that defiles me and begin to put on the fruit of forgiveness in my life. Please help me to restore and repair the relationships that I have wounded and destroyed by my bitterness. Thank You for Your great gift of grace to me. In Jesus' name. Amen!"

Forgiving others is not an option for the Christian; it's required, and it is step number one in removing bitterness.

"Since God chose you to be the holy people whom

He loves, you must clothe yourselves with tender-hearted mercy, kindness, humility, gentleness, and patience. You must make allowance for each other's faults and forgive the person who offends you. Remember, the Lord forgave you, so you must forgive others."Colossians 3:12-13 (NLT)

My words...

THIS IS WHAT I MUST WORK ON WITH GOD EACH DAY. I will be reminded and harassed by the devil. When I am, I will choose to remind myself I HAVE FORGIVEN THAT and will not let it come into me. BR

From article.....

"In forgiving others, it is important to remember a few important rules: When I forgive, I resolve never to bring this circumstance or situation up again to the one I forgave, to anyone else, or even to myself. It is a closed book. If you are going to pattern your forgiveness after that of the Lord, then you will choose to remember no more the sin committed against you."

My words...

I was raised by a mother who was full of bitterness toward her father, my grandfather. As I look back on my young life, it seems she protected her bitterness as something she had a rite to hold on to (I'm guilty of this with my wife). What I've learned from my mom's brother and sisters, my mother was physically and verbally abused by her father and possibly uncles. Although she was under psychiatric care and was a prescription drug addict for many of my growing-up years, she never found freedom from the bitterness she held on to. It deeply affected our home and my relationship with her. I grew up resenting what I saw in her and the way she treated me and my father. Many years later and after a long journey of gaining understanding, I have since forgiven my mother and I no longer hold hurts and unforgiveness against her. (This was the core of my inability to forgive, to relate, and respond in a healthy way to those *I loved*.)

Even though I was raised by an unforgiving bitter mother, she loved us kids and we knew it. But I saw, experienced, and learned the behavior of unforgiveness and bitterness from her. It's like an addiction, it's familiar and can be easy to fall back into. But Jesus is our victory and strength. He has paid for our sin, the sin of unforgiveness and bitterness. When the familiar sin of unforgiveness arises, I must practice over and over what Jesus does for me...FORGIVE, OVER AND OVER!!

01/09/21

I sat down with my wife and shared this with her. I did this out of obedience to God, for healing my heart, and from a desire to do my part in making things right with my wife. I read this word for word to her. I confessed my sin of unforgiveness toward her and the bitterness I was holding on to. I asked her to forgive me (she said she did) and I committed to practicing forgiveness with her.

I know this is not a one and done deal. One of the things the enemy loves to do is remind me of the hurts. They are still raw. But forgiveness says NO to the reminders. Forgiveness must be practiced every single day.

(God spoke this to me today 1/19/21. Read James 4, every night!)

To all God Made Men, the people in your life, parents, uncles, cousins, ministers, bosses, and SPOUSES that you are holding resentment and bitterness toward must be forgiven. You must bring this to God. Let Him speak to you and heal you, and then you must do what He tells you to do. If you don't, none of your relationships will be healthy, NONE. Bitterness will put you in a prison. You will look at every person in your life through those prison bars. Some of us believe we're not in this prison because we've "put the experience behind us." It's now so far behind us in our past that we are convinced we've done the hard work of forgiveness. All we've done is sweep it under the rug. You must allow God to show you where you are with Him and OTHERS. All others.

I truly thank God for all the hurt and pain of my last marriage, because it led me to face my sin of unforgiveness and so much more. I hate that we went through this, but it led me to where I am now, FREE of bitterness. My prayer is that you will come to God and yield to Him so He can heal your life.

CHAPTER 10

MY GREATEST LESSON (From my personal journal)

As I journeyed through my healing, God very tenderly began to show me my greatest lesson, my "mother and father wounds." Here's the thing, most humans carry emotional wounds from someone in their early life. It was about March of 2021 when God began to show me this. I'm convinced I would not have seen this if I hadn't first faced my bitterness. This journey was one of the most healing journeys that I've ever experienced. All of a sudden, I got clarity, understanding, and answers to questions I've been asking about myself for decades. I wanted to include this in the book because many men and women are wounded, and like me don't know what to do about it. I'm convinced God showed this to me for my complete healing and so I can talk about it with you. So again, I wrote it as it came. Here it is.

Soon to be seven years of marriage, seven years of counseling with eighteen counselors, some of which were individual counseling for both of us, have not been wasted on me. I've learned a lot about myself. As I reflect on it all, I'd say what I've learned about myself has been my biggest blessing.

As I've said before, I was raised by a very bitter, unforgiving, angry mother. I grew up resenting her outbursts and rage. In my later adult years I began to learn more about my mother. She was raised by a physically and emotionally abusive father, my grandfather. The stories I've heard are horrifying. It seems her and her youngest brother, my uncle, received the worst of the abuse. I learned more after visiting with him and my aunt in 2018.

My mother's anger and rage was imprinted on me all my growing-up years. In 2002 when my mother lay dying in a hospital, my sister called to tell me and said, "you need to come if you want to see her before she passes." I told her to let me know when she passes and I'll make arrangements to come to the funeral. I look back with regret on that. Many years later, God graciously walked me through that and I was able, for the first time, to forgive my mother and myself.

I have recently come to terms with another kind of behavior that I grew up under. One that I now believe has had the biggest and most profound negative impact on my life. Passivity, and a passive father. I never knew or understood this until now, many years later. This recent understanding has answered many questions about myself I've held on to for years.

HERES A DEFINITION OF PASSIVE:

"Receiving or subjected to an action without responding or initiating an action in return.

Accepting or submitting without objection or resistance; submissive:"

I grew up loving and admiring my father. I called him my Hero. He worked hard to provide for our family. Never did my brother and sister or I worry about being taken care of. He loved my mother and cared for her every need, or, so it seemed.

I now know my father behaved passively toward my mother. I saw it though, as a tremendous amount of love being shown to her. But, I began to see things that I didn't understand, and I became good at ignoring them. As I grew older it became more clear. I now realize my father did everything he could to please and appease my mother's every wish, desire, and demands. He did it to "keep the peace" in our home, and he did the same "balancing act" with mom in the churches he pastored. He tried hard to keep this from us kids. He did it later in life just to go from peace to peace for himself.

I know a lot about my mother's life as a child and an adult. I dug into it because I saw her as "my problem." I know nothing about my father's family life and childhood. I know why my mother lived in bitter unforgiveness toward her father. I know now why she behaved the way she did, but I don't know anything about what caused dad to be such a passive individual, other than the fact it's a trait in all men. I want to be clear about my father. He was the kindest most caring person I ever knew. All others loved him. But when it came to my mother, he gave in to her every demand. As a result she took advantage of him. I do know this, men are prone to be passive. We see it as early as Adam when he chose passivity and did not step in between Eve and the serpent. He chose compliant passivity again when he ate the fruit. Not only are these male traits, these behaviors are learned. They are imprinted in a person's psyche from early in life. So I can only assume my father learned this behavior as a boy growing up in his home. It was modeled in front of me all my growing up years.

I know this, dad gave in to my mother's every whim and want. Many times, not without an argument late at night while us kids were "asleep." But nonetheless, he would give in and always at a high cost.

Here's an example of the unstable demanding of my mother, and my father's passivity. My earliest childhood memory of our home/house was at around four or five years old. It was the only home dad ever built. A nice three bedroom brick home in 1960. My father was an electrician by trade. From the outside we seemed to be the typical middle class family living the dream. But inside, there was instability. But at my age I knew nothing and didn't know for years because dad was good at covering it up and protecting us.

I now know there was an unhealthy restlessness in my mother. And as the passive one, dad would give in. From my earliest memories to the day my mother passed in 2002, mom and dad lived in 15 houses, 3 states, 10 cities, and 6 different homes at different times in one city, and no they weren't military. Mom would become restless and want to move. Dad didn't want to but would give in to her manipulation and anger. Their last home was their longest and they were there for about 15 years. Mom hated it but her health was too bad to move again.

Another example. My mother was a prescription drug addict. As long as I can remember she was addicted to drugs, pain killers. I now know she was covering up her emotional pain. Because of my father's passivity he became her codependent enabler. It seems for 30 years or more mom saw a psychiatrist, which is how she got her drugs. Dad would give in to her drug addiction to the point that pharmacies stopped filling her prescriptions because they knew what was going on. I can still see the handful of various drugs dad would pour into her hand at her demand. My uncle, mom's brother, told me that dad was given the nick-name "St. Bobby" by the family because of how toler-antly passive he was with mom.

In my adult years I became more and more angry at my mother for the way she treated and took advantage of my father, and frustrated at my father for always giving in to her. So now I was seeing my dad as being abused, and my hero for taking the abuse. Some how I saw him as "being strong" for being able to endure. My love for him and my desire for him to have peace in life, blinded me to his lifelong learned behavioral flaw. His passivity became passive-aggressive, but I couldn't see it for my hatred of my mother's behavior and my love for my father and my desire for him to have the peace he longed for.

As I look over my life, my growing up years and my struggles with anger, my enjoyment of quiet and peace, my "being ok" with being alone, and my need to escape has become more clear to me.

It wasn't until 2014 after I married my second wife that all this began to make sense. In the middle of my own marital strife I started seeking understanding. I began to realize I had a huge bitterness problem toward my mother due to my choosing not to forgive her. I began to prayerfully work through this. Through counsel and seeking God's help, in 2018 I was able to finally forgive my mother. I understand her and I forgive her. God washed over me with His peace that covered all the years she was in my life until she passed in 2002.

My father passed in 2012. It wasn't until 2019 that I began to look deep into my relationship with my father and began to see the wound he put into me by what I learned and experienced with him. This was hard to except at first because of the love I have for my father, but I kept leaning into God. I know I carry a father wound. But I have to be honest with myself; as much as I loved and admired my father, my biggest relationship struggles, life failures as an adult, as a husband and father are rooted in the wounds I learned and received from him. I've lived my whole life until now without this understanding. I'm happy to see it now.

In my first marriage (27 years), I behaved outwardly like my mother—aggressive, controlling, loud, and demanding. I treated my wife and sons with controlling hostility. I was my mother to them. And here's the thing, I knew something was wrong in me but I didn't understand it. I was tormented on the inside for the way I treated them, but I had no clue what to do about it. I destroyed my wife's love for me and emotionally abused my two sons, especially my oldest son. I'M SO SORRY!! I realize there's some forgiveness work on myself I still need to do for this.

Here's where the understanding of my "father wound" now helps. I now realize what I was doing, why I was behaving the way I did. I now know *"I was not going to be like my father" and be passive.* I was not going to be "walked on" the way my father was. I was not going to "lose my controlling power over them and be controlled." I was the opposite of my father in my first marriage. I was my mother. If you had challenged me with that back then I would've denied it. My behavior killed my marriage, destroyed the heart of my wife, and damaged my sons (oh how I pray for them!). I now realize it was all because I was not going to be like my father and be walked on. I've never seen this until now, and I am thankful for the answers and this new understanding.

While married to my first wife in 2000, I stepped away from pastoring to try to save my marriage. For the next three years I tried to focus on saving my marriage but the damage had been done.

We divorced in 2003 after 27 years of marriage, and for the next 10 years I was single. In those ten years a change came over me. A good change. It was an experiential awakening of a whole new way of relating to people. For ten years I did not have an out-of-control conflict experience with anyone. During those ten years I had more people in my life than ever before. I had friends, good close friends, best friends. I was in a good church and small group weekly. I had a girlfriend. I lived a close interactive life with people without controlling or being controlled. I experienced no out of control anger with anyone. No conflicts. There were disagreements of course, but we worked it out. I became a different man in those ten years. I liked who I'd become, and I liked the peace that came with it.

In 2012 I recommitted my life to God and His call to preach and pastor. I was single and desperately wanted to be married again. I met my second wife in 2013 and we married in 2014. Even though I said I liked the man I had become, I still hadn't learned anything about my mother and father wounds. I brought both of them into my new relationship and marriage. But this time it was different. I was like my father, very passive. I now realize I wanted to continue to live in the peace I had known for the past ten years. My wife though, brought her own unhealed wounds into our marriage from her father, mother, and step-father, her first marriage, and the abuse of others in her childhood. Two terribly broken people coming together to form the "perfect storm." She was the aggressor, and I became my father, passive. As in my first marriage I chose not to lead as I should. I chose not to say no when I should've. Instead, I chose to give in, I chose surrender, I chose compliance in hopes of momentary peace. I remember thinking over again after another major conflict, "maybe this is the last time." Then, around 2019 I became like my mother, unforgiving, resentful, and bitter toward her for all her bad behavior, hurts, and words she said to me in our conflicts. Here's the truth. We both brought our learned imprinted behavior into this marriage, and to each other.

We were married for seven plus years. It was during our 2nd separation in 2021 that our seventh anniversary came and went. It's during this separation that I've come to terms with my father wound. I don't resent him, I never did. But I see it now, and I except it. Dad wounded me deeply and he nor I knew what was happening. God led me to see this and I have forgiven my father. I'm deeply thankful to God for revealing this to me. I can now experience complete healing.

I'm the oldest of three. Not sure if that means anything but it seems to me I got the worst of my father and mother. I also got their best. I never doubted my father's love for me. He showed me, he said it often. He demonstrated love to my mother in front of us kids. He showed it and said it often.

My mother loved me. I never doubted it but I was confused. She, at times, affectionately showed it and said it often. But they both brought their wounded brokenness into their marriage relationship. Sadly, they never found peace together.

Men, if you're carrying unhealed hurts with you from your past, you must seek help about this. Some of you have become very good at believing "you've forgiven" those who've wounded you. The fact is you've pressed it down and swept it away. But, those unhealed hurts continue to surface in your relationships, especially your marriage. You'll never be the man God has designed you to be until you face this. He will lead you to healing if you will open your heart to the truth about yourself.

CONCLUSION

I thank God that He turned me on to Genesis 1-3 again. I'm thankful to my friend Trampus for saying what he did at a time when I needed to hear it. It is time that men step up and become God's authentic man. There has never been a time when that is needed more than now. Men, I pray you have seen what your God-given role is. If you're married your wife needs you to be the sawhorse God made you to be so she can be the sawhorse He made her to be. Did you hear that? You must be the "God made man" He made you to be so she can be all that you need her to be. Listen men, God made your Eve to complement the man God created you to be. Anything less will suffer and most likely fail. If you are raising children, those boys and girls need you to lead, love, provide, and protect as God designed you to do. The answer to real manhood is found throughout God's word, but the foundation, the template for every man, woman, and marriage was forged in the beginning.

Men, God created you to be dependent on Him your whole life. He has a plan and a purpose for your life. Your effectiveness is seen in your dependence on God. Men are to be connected to God in every way. No matter what the culture says about men's and women's roles, it is what God says that matters.

Like Adam, build your relationship with God. Spend time with Him. Learn about Him. Allow Him to shape you into the man He wants you to be. Let Him lead you vocationally. If you're a fish in a tree find your water. If you're a young man your future family will depend on it. If you're older like me get a restart. It's never too late to do the right thing.

It's impossible to teach men their God given role using Genesis 1-3, without talking about the woman's role as well. For a man to understand his role he must understand hers. We are in this together. Women were created to be dependent on their husbands. I know that will be hard to hear for some but according to the biblical text, it's truth and it's still truth today. Their effectiveness is seen in their dependence on their husband. Eve was literally connected to Adam physically. In this lies one of the most significant biblical principles for every woman after Eve. Her worth and effectiveness is connected to her husband. Eve was made from a physical part of Adam that contained the life giving breath of God. Every man must understand this. Unfortunately, the great majority of women don't understand this, yet at the same time they will say yes to the man being connected to God and under submission to Him. If God can make him a better man then by all means women want their men to be better men. Ladies, the same biblical standard applies to you as well.

I know what I'm writing and I know it won't be well received by some men and women who are influenced by today's culture. But I believe it's biblical truth, and that is all that matters. The truth of what God says is needed in our culture today more than ever, and it must be led by real, authentic, godly men with the help and support of real, authentic, godly women. Like I continue to say to my John Wayne friends, "let's start being the difference that our culture desperately needs to see."

As I have written this book my prayer has been that God will use these words to reach into the heart of men. Men, God loves you and He loves the plan that He's created for you and your wife. But His plan requires that you become His God Made Man.

***

ACKNOWLEDGMENTS

I want to thank the many who read this book in order to help me with your thoughts, opinions, and suggestions. They were all considered seriously. What I liked most was the honest feedback I got from so many. I know not everyone will like this book because of the strong positions I take on cultural issues and you who read it were very clear on your likes and dislikes. For all your help, thank you.

CONTACT THE AUTHOR

www.bobbyrice.br@gmail.com

Made in the USA
Coppell, TX
28 November 2022

87278938R00090